Dialectical Behavioral Therapy

The Complete Guide to Living a Happier and Healthier Life

(Mindfulness and Emotion Regulation Techniques for Overcoming Stress)

Terry Morgan

Published By **Elena Holly**

Terry Morgan

All Rights Reserved

Dialectical Behavioral Therapy: The Complete Guide to Living a Happier and Healthier Life (Mindfulness and Emotion Regulation Techniques for Overcoming Stress)

ISBN 978-1-7772262-8-2

No part of this guidebook shall be reproduced in any form without permission in writing from the publisher except in the case of brief quotations embodied in critical articles or reviews.

Legal & Disclaimer

The information contained in this book is not designed to replace or take the place of any form of medicine or professional medical advice. The information in this book has been provided for educational & entertainment purposes only.

The information contained in this book has been compiled from sources deemed reliable, and it is accurate to the best of the Author's knowledge; however, the Author cannot guarantee its accuracy and validity and cannot be held liable for any errors or omissions. Changes are periodically made to this book. You must consult your doctor or get professional medical advice before using any of the suggested remedies, techniques, or information in this book.

Upon using the information contained in this book, you agree to hold harmless the Author from and against any damages, costs, and expenses, including any legal fees potentially resulting from the application of any of the information provided by this guide. This disclaimer applies to any damages or injury caused by the use and application, whether directly or indirectly, of any advice or information presented, whether for breach of contract, tort, negligence, personal injury, criminal intent, or under any other cause of action.

You agree to accept all risks of using the information presented inside this book. You need to consult a professional medical practitioner in order to ensure you are both able and healthy enough to participate in this program.

Table Of Contents

Chapter 1: Emotion Regulation 1

Chapter 2: Mindfulness And Emotions ... 27

Chapter 3: Interpersonal Effectiveness .. 39

Chapter 4: Distress Tolerance 57

Chapter 5: The Balance Between Two Extremes 77

Chapter 6: The Four Modules Of Dbt 97

Chapter 7: Skills Training And Practical Exercises 133

Chapter 8: The Role Of Dialectics In Dbt 156

Chapter 9: Integrating Dbt Into Everyday Life 163

Chapter 10: Implementing Dbt For Your Counseling Workout 176

Chapter 1: Emotion Regulation

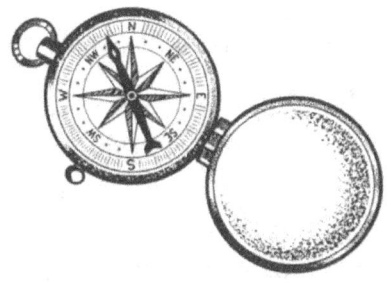

Let's begin this route expertise the regulation of feelings, how they seem, and why every now and then you are full of anger and act in a sure way; possibly you have got blamed yourself for saying some issue that harm some unique man or woman, however it is because of the fact you probably did now not recognize a way to alter your feelings or why it happened.

How Emotional Deregulation Manifests

Emotional self-regulation in young adults is a critical thing of emotional intelligence as it consists of developing the capability to govern your feelings, whether they may be great or painful, in preference to permitting them to dominate you.

Emotional strength of will refers back to the capability to maintain emotions within a certain variety of version to what's happening.

Having emotional electricity of mind manner you are aware of your emotions, express them, and apprehend the manner to control them nicely.

I recognize that feelings guide and condition behavior; for example, in case you are angry, involved, or stressful, you can have a tough time sitting down and mastering to calm down.

If you can't adjust feelings, you received't be capable of manipulate your behavior.

Behavior problems in children are regularly associated with problem regulating emotions appropriately.

The method of carrying out emotional self-regulation begins offevolved within the first months of life and keeps into adulthood. Everyone follows their personal direction to emotional maturity: some acquire it fast, at the identical time as others discover it extra tough. This approach of emotional and behavioral self-law is stimulated with the resource of severa factors:

Temperament is decisive in phrases of regulating emotions in the first months of lifestyles. Some infants are extra sensitive and intense to emotions together with soreness and feature a tougher time calming down, even as different infants, in the identical state of affairs, respond extra lightly and lighten up extra without issues. It's find it irresistible takes place to you as a youngster, you spot that others take matters with extra positivity than you or the opportunity manner spherical.

The surroundings performs an essential position in the acquisition of emotional self-law; I suggest, the feature of dad and mom as an outdoor regulator. When kids are greater younger, it's far the dad and mom who provide position models of a way to reply to and manipulate feelings, in particular folks who create soreness or frustration.

Neurodevelopmental Disorders (ADHD). In the case of ADHD (interest deficit hyperactivity disease), emotional dysregulation is a diagnostic function. Studies have proven neurobiological vulnerabilities in people with ADHD, with areas which includes the prefrontal cortex, amygdala, and nucleus accumbens regulating attention, impulsivity, and emotional states affected.

When kids discover ways to adjust their emotional responses, they end up loads a great deal less susceptible in stressful situations, are much more likely to have sufficient emotional belongings to preserve accurate arrogance, preserve healthful friendships, and feature a higher functionality to pay interest and study.

Emotional dysregulation includes trouble in coping with our emotions and conduct, manifested inside the propensity to enjoy intense emotions and trouble returning to a calm u.S. Of the united states.

Difficulties in self-emotional law in youngsters and children are specifically manifested in:

High degree of anxiety.

Low frustration tolerance.

Impulsive or disruptive behaviors.

Little flexibility.

Denial of unpleasant emotions consisting of worry, unhappiness, and pain.

Intense and commonplace tantrums.

The work includes, after exploring the reasons of emotional dysregulation, interventions that intention to reap better emotional law and manipulate thru the identity and entire expression of emotions, in particular the most powerful ones together with anger, frustration, sadness, and fear.

It is regularly difficult to manipulate impulses whilst there may be an emotional law trouble, so in treatment, it's far crucial to provide strategies to discover ways to manipulate it, as it may represent a problem that affects a more youthful individual in their own family and social environment or university existence.

Often, the intellectual strategies I will show you right here to deal with impulsivity, anger, melancholy, and strong or painful feelings are pretty essential inside the psychotherapeutic method.

Emotional self-regulation remedy for youngsters is individualized and looks at elements along with:

The own family surroundings

Possible related issues which incorporates ADD, oppositional defiant disorder, amongst others

Age

Personal inclinations

In all times, the priority is to make you aware that emotions which incorporates anger, frustration, and worry are natural and of the beside the point processes in which these emotions are displayed, i.E., unfavourable behavior inside the route of others or your self.

It can be very critical to discover ways to mirror on the results of impulsive reactions.

Different strategies are used to discover ways to control feelings and behavior, such as emotion-centered behavior manage techniques, play techniques, and relaxation strategies.

When youngsters are very younger, play strategies (video games, storytelling, drawing) are specifically used to alter feelings and conduct. In addition, interventions popularity on the want to offer mother and father with guidance to assist find effective procedures to deal with every different's behavior problems.

For younger people, psychotherapy in this example is especially based totally on a verbal exchange but moreover uses innovative strategies (narration, drawing, function performs, relaxation strategies).

Adolescent psychotherapy specializes in assisting them trade their hassle behaviors. To accumulate this, interventions are oriented to apprehend the emotional international of more youthful humans. Accepting in choice to averting emotional reviews is the first step in regulating feelings and behavior.

How to Navigate Your Emotions

How are you feeling proper now as you study this? Are you curious? Would you need to understand some issue approximately yourself? Are you bored because of some issue you need to do at university and you truely don't want to? Or are you glad because of the fact it's far your preferred school mission? Maybe you're distracted by using manner of different occasions, like waiting for plans for the weekend or feeling horrific approximately the breakup.

Emotions like the ones are part of being human. They provide information approximately what is taking place in the mean time and help you recognize a manner to answer.

Since formative years, we've emotions as I counseled you in advance than. Babies and infants reply to their feelings through facial expressions or moves collectively with guffawing, crying, or hugging. They express and experience emotions, despite the truth that they can't name the ones feelings or touch upon in which they arrive from.

As life is going through the usage of, we get better at expertise the manner it really works, and in place of reacting like kids, we're capable of see it as a sense and display it. Over time and with exercise, you can learn how to see the manner you feel and why. It is the functionality known as emotional reputation.

Emotional popularity serves to discover what we need and want. It enables to create more potent relationships. This is because of the reality feelings are understood and the feeling can be expressed surely, preserving off or resolving conflicts and overcoming feelings in a higher way.

Some people are more aware about what they revel in than others. The first-rate detail is that everybody can grow to be aware about what they revel in, it surely takes workout. But it's far proper that emotional interest is worked on so that emotional intelligence develops, it is a knowledge to help you to reach existence.

I will go away you some primary notions of feelings:

Emotions come and skip. Many dad and mom revel in numerous certainly one of a kind feelings in some unspecified time in the future of the day. Some final just a few seconds, and others may be extended and reason exceptional sentiments.

Emotions can be mild, robust, or in amongst. The depth of what you experience will rely on the situation and the character.

There are not any terrible or proper emotions, but there are horrible and top techniques to specific them (or act on them). Knowing a way to particular what we experience is a separate skill, that's based totally surely at the know-how of feelings.

If you feel anger, unhappiness, or a cocktail you don't recognize how to name, that's first-rate.

Some emotions are great: which includes feeling satisfied, loved, stimulated, assured, happy, thankful, fascinated, or protected. Other emotions may appear extra bad: like feeling angry, accountable, afraid, green with envy, ashamed, concerned, or unhappy. Both advantageous and terrible feelings are ordinary.

All emotions say something approximately yourself and your scenario. But every so often it may appear difficult with a purpose to acquire those emotions. You can determine your self primarily based totally on fantastic feelings, along with whilst you feel jealous. But rather than wondering which you shouldn't experience this way, it's higher to apprehend how you sense.

Trying to keep away from negativity or pretending you're not sorry can backfire. Difficult emotions are more hard to triumph over and can leave in case you don't face them and try and recognize why you revel in the way you do. You don't have to stay on the way you experience or talk about your emotions constantly. Emotional awareness in reality method respecting, recognizing, and accepting what you're experiencing.

Create Emotional Awareness

Emotional popularity allows you understand and receive yourself. How do you turn out to be more aware about what you enjoy? Get commenced with those easy steps:

1.   Seek to research how you're in severa conditions at some degree in the day and make this a every day workout. You might also additionally experience excited after making plans to transport somewhere at the side of your buddies. Or in all likelihood you experience involved earlier than an exam. Perhaps you experience calm at the same time as listening to tune, inspired whilst you go to see some thing that appeals to you need a skateboarding game, or happy even as a pal congratulates you.

2.   Just see any emotion that entails you and provide it a name in your head. It will most effective take a 2d to try this, however it's a excellent exercising. You will find out that with every emotion that passes, it leaves an area for the subsequent revel in.

3.   Evaluate the depth of this feel. Once you've positioned and named an emotion, circulate one step similarly: Rate the way you experience about that sensation on a scale of one to ten, with 1 being the least excessive and 10 being the simplest depth.

4.   Share what you sense with those close to you. It is the first-rate manner to exercising and learn how to located emotion into verbs, a ability to help you get towards those you like as pals, boyfriends or girlfriends, dad and mom, coaches, and anyone else round you. Make sharing your emotions with pals or circle of relatives a each day workout. You can percentage a few element very personal, or certainly some thing that took place to you.

Four Coping Techniques of Emotion Regulation

I will leave you these techniques to deal with the law of feelings. Then, within the subsequent issue, I will educate you to address your self step by step.

Take the Time to Understand What You Are Feeling

If the struggle does now not require instantaneous hobby, attempt to discover an area wherein you could relax.

Breathe slowly and try to recognize a number of the simple feelings that I confirmed you.

You mustn't make rate judgments together with "I want to no longer experience this manner," go through in mind that this is an automatic response, and be aware for your self.

Later you can decide if it's miles available to specific it and the manner.

Own What You Feel

A very common mistake is to use the phrase "You make me enjoy this way."

This is frequently controversial because it denies our duties.

You need to well known your subjective mind and interpretations that arouse feelings no matter the moves of others.

It is higher to apply "When you try this, I feel…"

Use the Right Words

If you use sensible verbs like: "I observe," "I understand," and "I enjoy," they don't rush to refute subjects due to the fact they test with an inner state of the person.

Only you understand how you enjoy. Convey the message as appropriately as possible.

Saying "I feel unique/lousy" can supply a complicated concept approximately your country of mind.

It is probably beneficial if you may issue to the decision of the emotion you recognized, or at least as close to as possible.

Analyze the Context

To do this, it is important to use empathy, that is, attempt to apprehend the emotions of the alternative character.

If you want to talk some thing you discovered may additionally moreover have a sturdy emotional effect at the opportunity individual, by no means do it at an beside the factor time and place, along with at the same time as using or on the brink of go out on a date.

The more touchy the facts, the more critical it's far that the receptor is in a snug surroundings and has an idea of the situation.

If it's no longer the right time to speak, don't permit time pass indefinitely, try and cheer your self up.

Laugh out loud, cry your disappointment, and specific your anger through sports that don't harm others or your self.

Do it everyday in conjunction with your man or woman and ideals. You can be sure that it's miles a step towards a fuller existence.

These techniques are useful for regulating your emotions and, blended with self-self perception, sell healthful and useful relationships.

I near this situation depend with a treasured reflection:

"When we can not trade the situation we're dealing with, the assignment is to exchange ourselves."

Emotional Regulation Exercises (Easy Step-By-Step Exercises)

Now pay interest and get in a function for us to do the ones emotional law carrying activities. Keep them handy while you feel feelings overwhelm you and get out of manipulate.

Deep Breathing

This is an emotion manage technique very easy to apply and additionally very useful for controlling physiological responses earlier than, in the direction of, and after managing emotionally traumatic situations. It is completed as follows:

1. Take a deep breath while counting in your thoughts to four.

2. Hold your breath as you rely to four yet again.

3. Breathe out at the same time as mentally counting to 8.

4. Repeat the above method.

In short, it has to do with doing the simplest-of-a-kind levels of breathing slowly and a hint more excessive than normal, but without forcing it at any time. To test which you are respiration effectively, you can region one hand on the chest and the other on the belly. When you breathe really put off your hands from your belly and you may breathe successfully. Also known as belly respiration.

Stop Thinking

If we're talking approximately strategies for dealing with emotions, this workout additionally can be used in advance than, all through, or after the situation that reasons you conflict. Specifically, it focuses on perception manipulate. To positioned it into exercising, you need to study the ones steps:

1. Pay hobby to the kinds of thoughts you have got whilst you start to feel uncomfortable, stressful, or confused, and apprehend any thoughts that have bad connotations (attention on failure, hatred of others, guilt, and so on.).

2. Tell yourself "Enough!"

3. Replace the ones thoughts with greater exceptional ones.

The hassle with this approach is that it takes a bit of exercise to perceive poor mind and turn them into immoderate terrific ones.

Muscle Relaxation

This emotional self-regulation technique may be performed in advance than, inside the course of, and after some situations, but its effective use requires training beforehand. If you want to location it into exercising, the ones are the stairs to conform with:

1. Sit flippantly in a cushty characteristic. Close your eyes.

2. Gradually loosen up all the muscle groups to your frame, beginning collectively along with your feet after which working your way up your body till you reach your neck and head muscle tissue.

3. Once you loosen up all the muscle businesses on your body, keep in mind a non violent and relaxing location, as an instance, laying on the seaside. Whichever area you choose out out, do not forget yourself in reality comfortable and carefree.

4. Imagine yourself in that area as in reality as possible.

Practice this exercise as long as you could, at the least as quickly as an afternoon for about 10 mins. If you have were given already were given the conviction of the usefulness of this workout, keep in mind that you want to exercise it to automate the machine and lighten up in seconds.

Mind Rehearsal

This is a few distinctive emotion manage technique designed for use earlier than going via a state of affairs in that you experience insecure. It includes without a doubt imagining that you are in that situation—as an instance, asking a person out with you—and you are doing a splendid hobby while feeling completely comfortable and assured.

You have to mentally exercising what you're going to mention and what you are going to do. Repeat severa times till you begin to revel in greater cushty and confident.

Thought Regulation

When you're confronted with a second of highbrow pain and don't understand a way to take care of your feelings, you often enjoy some component called "raced questioning." Many instances, those uncontrolled thoughts are negative and do not will assist you to find answers to worrying situations.

For the identical reason, idea regulation can be an powerful emotion control technique. What have to you do? The first step is probably to encounter the flow into of mind and decide what type arises for your head. Next, if you are by myself, you may strive writing them in a pocket book after which processing the statements.

Logic Reasoning

Logical reasoning is closely associated with the previous emotional control strategies, which consist of reading one after the other the mind that purpose you emotional pain and logical reasoning. Here is an example of the manner to do it:

1. You suppose: "I am useless and worthless."

2. Emotion: You cry and are sad.

3. Logical reasoning: "How actual is all this? What true is it for me to assume all this? What can I do to forestall thinking this manner?"

Distraction

Emotional management talents additionally include ways to deal with emergencies, even as you cannot otherwise control your emotions. When you enjoy overwhelmed through emotions, you may attempt to distract yourself with some comforting stimulus, together with a tune, a ebook, a movie, and so on.

Self-Regulation

Emotional self-law is a completely effective approach you need to workout to govern your emotions. To obtain this manner, the following steps are required:

1. Detect and component out moments at the same time as you lose control.

2. As you loosen up out, reflect onconsideration on the triggers for the scenario (what you've got been thinking about while you out of place manage of your feelings).

3. Identify triggering mind before they convey approximately uncontrollable emotions.

four. Learn to adjust your feelings in moments of catastrophe with the help of different relaxation techniques.

These are the respiration wearing activities that you may do in this example:

Abdominal Inspiration

The motive of this exercising is to preserve the inhaled air to the lowest of the lungs. For it:

1. One hand must be located at the stomach and the other at the belly.

2. In practice, at the same time as breathing with the hand at the stomach, you

want to enjoy the movement, now not the hand on the stomach.

3. Breathe inside and outside feeling it this way.

It may also additionally moreover appear hard at the start, but it's a trick that could take 15-20 mins.

Abdominal and Ventral Inspiration

The objective is to learn how to direct the inhaled air inside the course of the lower and center zones of the lungs. Same due to the truth the previous exercising, however as quickly because the lower element is filled in, the center location ought to furthermore be stuffed in. Attention want to be paid first to the movement of the hand at the stomach, and then to the machine of respiratory.

Chapter 2: Mindfulness And Emotions

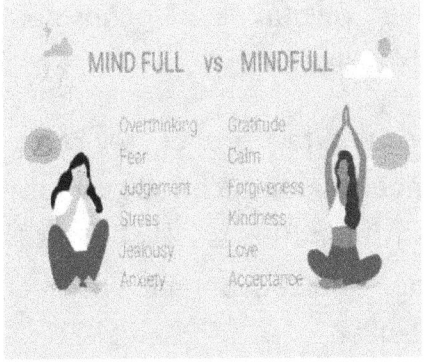

An incredible device that will help you deal with your feelings is mindfulness. I will show you on this chapter the way it virtually works and the assist it is able to give you.

What Is Mindfulness?

The benefits of mindfulness are very famous.

A quick are seeking on the Internet can show all its awesome capability for enhancing the manner you address stress, set dreams, artwork via depressive symptoms and symptoms, or even find out because of this and satisfaction in existence.

Furthermore, the ones claims are supported with the resource of considerate and replicable research.

However, it's far proper to recognize the which means and technological statistics at the back of mindfulness. How does it have an effect on and advantage intellectual and bodily health?

In this chapter, we cross in addition into this. We may have a study the due to this of mindfulness, its psychology, and its software program in areas of our lives.

Mindfulness (or sampajañña in Pali), one of the most important languages of the Buddhist scriptures, way clean information. The definition is regular with its purpose, helping you see extra certainly, deal successfully with what life also can throw at you, and in the long run make more informed options.

When used, mindfulness frequently denotes a country of mind: The feeling of calm, gratitude, and compassion which could have a profound impact on you.

When used as a verb, as an example, "conscious," it has to do with entering into that u.S.A., practising a way of being in the gift. The moment of awareness turns into a 2nd of tenderness and take care of your emotions, thoughts, and bodily sensations. Research helps anecdotal evidence that gaining a aware mind can lead to a happier, extra inexperienced life.

Although mindfulness has its roots in historical Chinese medication, in today's years it's been considerably finished to fashionable Western healing procedures to deal with many highbrow and physical conditions.

After all, mindfulness education improves intellectual hobby and alters the connections inside the thoughts and bodily methods.

It works speedy, best five classes are had to beautify the essential and autonomic worried systems, which can be needed to regulate involuntary physical capabilities, work thru strain and hazard, and the connection among the thoughts and our inner structures. Connections are crucial.

Deeply rooted in the concept and the which means that of mindfulness, it is tested that we aren't some aspect consistent on the brain diploma, that is, that if we've were given a manner of being, it is not like that and that's it, in distinct phrases, we're "neuroplastic." This is what neuroscientists name our capability to look at, unlearn, and expand. Imagine the mind inner full of many connections, at the same time as you're making adjustments, new connections are long-established, they call that neuroplasticity.

The idea that your brain is constantly changing sooner or later of your life approach that your experience of properly-being, contentment, and awesome existence may be altered by way of the manner you revel in the prevailing second.

Mindfulness Psychology

Shauna Shapiro, who has researched and written significantly on mindfulness and the way to conceptualize it, says, "Mindfulness is more than simply focusing."

It has to do with paying interest. Three essential highbrow factors of mindfulness are described in this way:

Intention: How you operate your coronary heart as a compass to manual and replicate your personal hopes and values.

Attention: Train and make stronger the mind in the gift second.

Attitude: Pay interest with compassion and interest.

Psychology indicates that mindfulness allows you escape of the cycle of horrible wondering, permitting you to "free your self from terrible self-speak" and reactive impulses and feelings.

After all, if you may't prevent the triggers of unsightly or annoying recollections, vital wondering styles, and awful self-communicate noise, you may select out what occurs subsequent. Mindfulness offers a pause, a reset, and every other way of searching at ourselves and our environment, shifting from "doing" to "being."

Then the mind can do extra than assume: You can emerge as aware of your thoughts. This presence, or metacognition permits you enjoy the arena extra right now and with less prejudice. You will discover the arena with eyes huge open, with high extraordinary emotions, amazed, dazzled, and thankful. It encourages you to enter a amazing upward spiral.

According to the American Psychological Association (APA), research suggests that on the identical time as not simply understood, the advantages of mindfulness come from its capacity to help us "lessen our body's response to strain" (American Association of Psychology, 2019, paragraph 10).

It seems that thru converting interest in mind regions associated with the law of attention and emotions, mindfulness can lessen the pressure response, that could have tremendous outcomes at some point of the body.

Modifying the way we act, even risky or unhelpful behavior, is regularly complex and appears to be past our conscious control. After all, in accordance to investigate, interest isn't a crucial situation for conduct or a precursor to conduct exchange.

Mindfulness gives a solution through unconsciously changing the manner you don't forget you studied, revel in, and behave. This exercising has been proven to help people who want to lessen or prevent smoking and eating via the usage of improving the method of self-interest of concept styles, that is frequently lacking in addicts.

How Can Mindfulness Help with Emotional Regulation?

As Martin Seligman (regularly hailed as the daddy of immoderate first-rate psychology) advises, high-quality psychology want to keep to comply beyond "from the neck up" to include and integrate the complete organism.

This trade and inclusion have brought approximately the involvement of many up to date neurofeedback and recovery techniques, which encompass mindfulness and biofeedback, which may be proving quite a success in treating anxiety and distinct issues associated with horrible highbrow fitness.

Mindfulness also can completely assist and make a contribution to great psychology, promoting a focus on pleasant feelings like gratitude and compassion. Mindfulness and meditation assist to reflect on feelings and mind in a sustained manner; this may inspire a shift from terrible emotions to more outstanding ones to heighten the enjoy of horrible feelings.

As with high exceptional psychology, mindfulness allows with reputation and recognition that feelings are regularly stimulated by using way of way of bodily sensations and acknowledges that even the maximum distressing feelings are brief: They are painful results that usually lessen or alternate through the years.

There is increasing proof that mindfulness exercising results in adjustments in u . S . A . And tendencies. Mindfulness meditation is given within the contemporary enjoy of in short changing the situation, wiring, and hobby sorts of the thoughts. However, with the longest engagement, the ones techniques can adjust your inclination towards mindfulness itself and make small adjustments to your personality.

Intervention programs have been correctly created that combine the techniques and targets of top notch psychology with mindfulness. One, created by way of Itai Ivtzan and friends, combines insights from "better self" interventions with mindfulness meditation practices to attention on methods to create a greater meaningful lifestyles.

Mindfulness will permit you to higher manage emotional states by way of way of calming down. Research indicates that at the same time as you exercising mindfulness in the context of meditative breathing (taking the time to breathe deeply and paying complete interest to how your breath feels inside the present moment), it may help lower your coronary coronary heart rate and boom your experience of protection, consequently transferring the thoughts a ways from combat, flight, and freeze modes that deprive better cognitive capabilities. When you've got got peace of thoughts, you may suppose in reality, so you are not overwhelmed with the beneficial aid of emotional urges.

Second, mindfulness lets in you increase abilties like controlling interest, self-consciousness, and metacognition, walking the intellectual muscle groups worried in emotional maturation and self-regulation.

Another way wherein you can paintings mindfulness to assist emotional self-law is via manner of growing the gap some of the stimulus and the way you respond. Research indicates that what's felt is constantly skilled first within the body in advance than it's miles diagnosed by using the conscious aspect. For instance, resentment can feel like a stressful neck, fear can sense like a racing coronary heart, and tension can show up as an accelerated rate of respiratory. Because of this connection amongst feelings and body shape, gaining 2d-thru way of-second popularity of the body and how it feels (mindfulness) can serve to offer you early caution of processes your emotions are brought on. This warning opens an opportunity to workout emotional strength of will and ask your self what's the healthiest reaction, in area of waiting for emotions to crush you. As Viktor Frankl observes, "There is an opening the numerous stimulus and the response." In that location, you may pick out out out your responses, which can be boom and freedom.

A fourth way that mindfulness can help alter feelings is provided with the resource of Dr. Ron Siegel inside the Science of Mindfulness video. Dr. Siegel, an assistant professor of clinical psychology at Harvard Medical School, explains that we regularly reply to emotional distress thru doing topics that make us experience happier, thereby decreasing the depth of pain and pain. Mindfulness does the alternative, improving your functionality to cope with bodily and emotional discomfort. When your capacity to address emotional distress will increase, you're loads less probably to answer to emotions or allow them to manipulate you.

Chapter 3: Interpersonal Effectiveness

To manage relationships efficiently, you want to realise about interpersonal effectiveness. In this bankruptcy, I will talk about it.

What Is Interpersonal Effectiveness?

In relationships, you often have abilties however you may moreover be too quick due to impulsiveness, low shallowness, uncontrollable emotional responses, belief patterns that don't artwork, and the insupportable pain of fear, anger, tension, or frustration, whilst, as an example, a courting ends. Your interpersonal war selection talents save you you from turning probably conflictive situations into excellent ones.

In phrases of the effectiveness of your dating, you typically commonly have a tendency to oscillate among avoiding conflict or going all-in. To be powerful, you require the self assurance to solve interpersonal and social conflicts and exchange the aversive environment to accumulate your dreams in interpersonal interactions. Necessary abilties are those who maximize a person's opportunities of carrying out desires in a given state of affairs without compromising relationships or recognize for that man or woman. Important: Take care of relationships; stability priorities with wishes in lifestyles and relationships; balance duty/preference ratios in life and relationships; generate a experience of competence and private admire.

Interpersonal efficacy applied to relationships consists of putting in vicinity or retaining top notch relationships, acting in this kind of manner that the opposite individual continues to love you and understand you, and locating a balance among our instant goals and the surrender of the connection inside the long term.

Myths about interpersonal effectiveness:

Whatever; I don't truly care.

I need to be willing to sacrifice myself for others.

I must be incompetent if I can't restoration it myself.

Saying "no" to a request is constantly selfish.

I don't deserve what I want or need.

I can't stand someone being mad at me.

The trouble is in my head. If I belief otherwise, I wouldn't need to hassle all of us.

Asking is for impolite human beings.

If they inform me "no" I will die.

If I ask for some factor, it's far going to reveal that I am a completely inclined person.

I want to recognise if a person is going to say sure in advance than I ask them for some component.

Effectiveness in keeping the relationship.

The abilities to be fostered are:

Be exceptional to people. Use a courteous and calm approach.

Do now not verbally or physical attack, or any of its variations.

Don't threaten. Do now not make manipulative statements or cowl threats. We want to tolerate rejected requests. Let's stay in this example, although it hurts. Run far from the state of affairs if vital.

Do not choose.

Take an interest in others. Listen and preserve interest in the amazing character. Don't interrupt or argue. Be touchy to the alternative person's desires. Be affected man or woman.

Learn approximately the other person's feelings, hobbies, problems, and angle at the scenario. Don't determine others.

Be empathetic and kind. Use humor and smile. Reassure the opportunity birthday celebration.

The manual proposed via the usage of the usage of Dialectical Behavioral Therapy for a behavior exchange is the subsequent:

Educate your self on the skills you want to analyze and why they will be essential.

Review interpersonal effectiveness goals.

Explain the connection a number of the varieties of validity.

Give examples of situations and goals.

Study the elements that lessen interpersonal effectiveness.

Understand the myths about interpersonal effectiveness.

Practice encouraging affirmations of the effectiveness of relationships.

Review the options to mild the electricity of the request or deny it and the elements that need to be taken into consideration in making the choice.

Learn the way to get what you need.

Know the manner to maintain relationships.

Know the manner to maintain personal admire.

How to Communicate Effectively

Now permit's see how you may particular your self, recognize how to mention "no" with out offending a few other person, and a manner to specific your emotions, especially folks who appear to get caught to your throat.

How to Speak for Yourself and Express Your Needs (Put Your Emotions into Words)

Trust is a wholesome shape of verbal exchange. It is the capability to shield yourself with honesty and recognize. Daily, you are confronted with situations in which you need self perception, and a experience of self-guarantee is probably of top notch assist; as an instance, at the same time as you ask a person out, ask a instructor a query or go to an interview approximately some component or communicate to a person crucial.

Not absolutely everyone is born assured. Some communicate too passively. Others stay a fashion with aggressiveness. The correct fashion is which you have a stability among the 2.

Being secure approach the following:

You can say "no" without guilt.

You can defend others.

You can specific your warfare of phrases respectfully.

You can explicit what you agree with you studied or the way you're.

You can endorse topics or make your thoughts seemed.

You can ask for what you need or want.

Why it's miles vital?

Communicating with self warranty permits you do what you need to do, however now not exquisite that. When you have got got were given self notion in your self, you recognize your self and others.

Those who specific themselves with self perception display that they may be assured in what they do. They are neither too shy nor competitive. They realise that what they assume and experience is well worth it. They are confident.

Confident humans generally generally tend to make buddies extra without troubles. They admire the wishes of others as an awful lot as their personal after they communicate. They are generally top at resolving disagreements and conflicts. They appreciate each one of a kind.

Do you have hundreds of passivity? Suffer aggression? Or have you ever ever found the steadiness?

How do you realise where you are at the safety and keep in mind scale? Here are some examples:

Paula's fashion has pretty some passivity. If you had been to invite Paula what movie she desired to look, she could in all likelihood probably say, "I don't understand, what do you need to look?" Most of the time, she we could others make the choice, however later she regrets now not expressing her goals. Their pals talk maximum of the time and that they annoy her. But at the same time as she attempts to join the communication, she speaks so softly that the others don't hear her and talk on the same time.

Jenny's style is actually too competitive. Jenny can speak her mind with out hesitation. But at the same time as she does, she comes inside the path of as harsh and dogmatic. She is on pinnacle of things of the verbal exchange, interrupting maximum of the time and seldom being attentive to others. If she disagrees with someone, she says so, typically with contempt or sarcasm. She has a reputation for being bossy and insensitive.

Ben is confident. When requested to particular his opinion, he is open and sincere. If he does not agree, he says so; but he does so without making subjects disrespectful or expressing himself to make others or himself feel lousy. Ben is inquisitive about being attentive to the opinion of others. He listens to what others want to mention. Even if he doesn't bear in mind a few issue, he despite the fact that respects the point of view of others.

The Sin of Passivity

People who behave too passively regularly grow to be being taken advantage of via others. They may additionally additionally furthermore enjoy damage, indignant, or inexperienced with envy.

Others can't recognise or apprehend you as masses as you do if you do now not specific your mind and emotions. This institution will not gain out of your contributions or your mind.

If you start to sense like your reviews or emotions don't matter, you can lose self assurance in your self and not have the opportunity to be identified and preferred on your particular mind. This can cause a depressed mood.

The Sin of Aggressiveness

People who speak aggressively also can moreover have a tough time making friends. They also can dominate the communique or specific their evaluations too forcefully and exceedingly, leaving others feeling rejected or angry.

People with an competitive style can get others to do things the manner they need, however in many cases, they end up being rejected or belittled. Others often stop respecting them.

Why Do We Lack Confidence?

Why are folks who communicate optimistically even as others seem passive or competitive? In thing, that is simply because of the way all and sundry is. It moreover has to do with the conduct they expand or the evaluations they go through. But, beyond that, they learn how to be assertive, terrible, or competitive once they see the behavior of others, in particular folks who train them.

Here are a few subjects which can have an impact on human beings to be passive:

Lack of self-self assure or appreciation for his or her opinion.

Worrying an excessive amount of about captivating others or a cherished one.

Worrying that others will now not accept as authentic with or reject their mind or evaluations.

Sensitivity to grievance or hurt with the aid of manner of stories from the day past in which their mind had been rejected or ignored.

There aren't any abilities to construct self-self guarantee.

Here are a number of the strategies human beings are endorsed to behave too aggressively:

Feeling too assured.

Too an entire lot popularity on assembly their dreams and displaying their critiques.

Not reading to comprehend or don't forget the opinions or goals of others.

They do no longer learn how to pay attention or ask for reviews from others.

What can lead humans to act with self belief (take the right steps) is the following:

Self-self perception.

They recall their opinions, their mind, and their feelings consider, and that they have the right to show what they've got.

They are robust (capable of accept complaint, rejection, and setbacks).

They understand the picks and goals of others.

They understand that their thoughts had been well-known or favored inside the past.

Ways You Can Build Confidence

To gain self notion, you want to have conversation skills and the right inner thoughts-set.

Some humans are virtually higher at projecting self belief. Others want greater exercise. But we are able to all beautify.

Here is the way to do it:

Start by thinking about which way of communique (aggressive, passive, or assured) is most like you. Then decide in case you need to artwork on being much much less passive or lots a good deal much less competitive, or if you really need to get into your in reality assured style.

If you want to work to be much less passive and extra assertive:

Pay hobby for your mind, the manner you enjoy, what you need, and what you like. You should be aware of all this earlier than showing it to others.

See in case you say "I don't understand," "I don't care," or "Okay" even as someone asks you what you need. Practice expressing your possibilities, specially close to the little records. For instance, if someone says, "Do you want black or red?" you could say, "I like blue, thanks."

Rehearse your feedback. For example, "Can you pass me a plate?" "I need a brush, do you've got were given every other?" "Can I actually have an area?" This permits you to ask for greater essential topics when you have to location your talents to apply.

Express what you suspect. Say if you desired the film you saw and why.

Practice using the phrase "I" in exceptional expressions. "I want..." "I determine upon..." "I think..."

Look for models who are self-assured, and who aren't so passive or competitive. See if you have the electricity to imitate the characteristics of the one you observe.

Remember that your thoughts and reviews have as an entire lot price as that of others. Knowing this can help you enjoy constant and confident in yourself. Confidence starts with an inner thoughts-set of valuing your self as you cost others.

If you need to paintings to reduce aggressiveness and be self-confident, I advocate:

Try to allow others to talk first.

See if you are taken into consideration considered one of those who interrupts. Stop and say: Sorry, pass on! And permit the character to complete.

Ask others what they suppose and concentrate to what they may be saying.

When you don't suppose the identical manner, attempt to explicit it without refuting what the alternative individual thinks. For instance, in region of pronouncing, "That's such an idiotic concept," simply say, "Actually, I don't accept as true with that idea." Or in choice to pronouncing, "He's an asshole," strive announcing, "I suppose he lacks insensitivity."

Look for models who are self-assured, neither too passive nor too aggressive. See if you can imitate the better tendencies of others.

Even oldsters which are pretty assured can enhance their capabilities. Work to beautify your fashion of talking actually:

Find models which have self-self perception, and aren't so passive or aggressive. See if you may imitate the outstanding of these. (As you could see, that is the equal advice I deliver to individuals who are too passive or too aggressive. It's due to the reality even a assured person doesn't forestall gaining knowledge of.)

Pay interest to what makes you feel maximum regular. The behavior of people varies from one situation to each distinctive. Many humans discover it easy to be assertive in some conditions, which includes with friends, but it becomes extra tough in different conditions, which includes with instructors or a person they've got definitely met. On more complicated topics, try and suppose, "What may I say to folks that are near me?"

Chapter 4: Distress Tolerance

We cannot keep away from feeling struggling and frustration at a few moments in lifestyles. The crucial thing is to realize a manner to art work those feelings and learn how to channel them. I will permit you to recognise approximately it on this chapter.

What Is Distress Tolerance?

Sometimes we have were given troubles which might be absolutely out of our manage. It's easy to think "it's no longer straightforward" or "I shouldn't have this problem," despite the fact that the ones mind simplest make the ache worse. Radical reputation refers to adopting a extra wholesome mindset within the ones conditions. Instead of specializing in the manner you would really like things to be unique, you widely known and be given a trouble or state of affairs for what it's far. Remember that accepting is not the same as searching or approving of something. By mastering to genuinely take delivery of issues which can be out of your control, you could experience a good buy a good deal less tension, anger, and disappointment even as handling them.

Teenagers exposed to violence are at elevated chance for max forms of psychopathology, consisting of melancholy, tension, and alcohol abuse. Research has recognized emotional reactivity and trouble regulating feelings as applicable mechanisms linking publicity to violence with psychopathology. Few studies have tested behavioral responses to distress as a mechanism for this association.

How to Experience Your Feelings Without Acting on Them

Emotions (emotions) are a few element commonplace and vital in our each day life we continuously go through.

Some feelings are remarkable. Imagine happiness, hobby, pride, enthusiasm, gratitude, hobby, and love. These emotions will can help you revel in cushty. On the alternative hand, terrible emotions which include sadness, loneliness, self-grievance, jealousy, anger, fear, or rejection may be complicated and painful.

You have to pay interest even as a terrible emotion is felt very often, with excessive intensity, or whilst it is processed for a long time.

Negativity cannot be avoided. We all revel in it from time to time. Negative emotions may also additionally have their complexity, however we will learn how to control them.

Here are three steps to help you manipulate horrible emotions.

First Step: Identify What You Feel

Knowing a way to be aware and understand what you feel calls for exercise. In addition to paying attention to the way you enjoy, take note of the way you enjoy bodily. Perhaps, with fine feelings, you have got were given physical sensations, you could feel a burning sensation on your face or annoying muscle organizations.

Pay attention to the way you enjoy. When you have horrific feelings, like anger, attempt naming your emotions.

For instance:

That man from my study club, Ian, simply drives me nuts collectively alongside along with his techniques!

I get so jealous once I see him/her with my ex.

Every time I flow close to the ones thugs, I get scared.

Stop denying your feelings. Maybe you don't want to inform others how you feel (like your ex or that individual for your have a observe club who scared you). But don't repress what you revel in. Simply naming those emotions is a exceptional deal better than pretending they don't exist (or mindlessly exploding).

Try to discover why you enjoy the manner you do. Think about what took place to make you feel this way.

For example:

Every time I do a assignment with my friends, John exhibits a way to stroll away with credit score score score for the art work absolutely everyone installed.

The instructor thinks that John is the great inside the magnificence, no matter the truth that he in no manner has specific thoughts; he steals ours.

If I see my ex who flirts with others, I find out that I'm despite the fact that in love.

Even despite the fact that the ones thugs don't even observe me, I see what they do to other humans and that's wherein my fear comes from.

Don't search for a person responsible. Identifying and explaining what you experience isn't just like blaming a few different man or woman or some difficulty on your emotions. Your ex may not have seen that different people make you revel in terrible, and the pal who receives all of the credit score for your work may not even understand he's doing it. When those objects show up, your emotions come from within. There's a cause you enjoy this way, which enables you understand what's taking area.

Accept that what you enjoy as feelings are natural and understandable. Stop judging your self through the emotions you feel. Assume they're a ordinary part of you. Recognizing your emotions allows you get over it; therefore, prevent treating yourself harshly.

Step Two: Take Action

Once you machine your emotions, you can determine in case you need to specific your emotions. Sometimes absolutely noticing the way you revel in is sufficient, but it moreover takes place that you want to do topics to experience higher.

Think of the fantastic manner to show your feelings. Is it time to be well mannered to someone else? Do you need to speak to a chum approximately the manner you experience? Or is it higher to move for a jog to launch your emotions?

For example:

I received't resolve anything via displaying my displeasure to John. I can also additionally even enjoy superior, however my emotions dictate that I want to keep away from being in some different scenario in which he assumes he's on top of things.

I'm going to reveal myself sturdy within the front of my ex. Then, I'm going to place on sad songs and, in my room, I'm going to launch what I feel after which turn the web page.

The worry I experience of being close to those thugs is an indication that they have come an extended way. Maybe I need to speak to someone in authority approximately it.

Work on information the way to exchange, the way you experience. The time will come while you want to move from a awful usa of the us of thoughts to a excellent one. Otherwise, you can reflect onconsideration on how awful subjects are, at the way to make you experience horrible. Try to do what fills you with happiness, even in case you don't sense find it impossible to resist at the time. For instance, you can not want to exit after a dating ends, however putting out with a friend or seeing a humorous film will make you sense higher.

Promote powerful emotions. These are those that supply us a sense of well-being and satisfaction. Get inside the dependancy of spotting the extraordinary matters in lifestyles and focusing on them (even the little matters, like your dad's reward for tidying up your library or the scrumptious salad you made for lunch). Focusing at the great, even while you're feeling down, will help you go from right all the way down to glad.

Ask for assist. Talk approximately the manner you experience about your mother and father, trusted adults, or friends. They will let you study your emotions and make you be aware subjects in some other way. There isn't anything that would make you feel better than even as a person you want allows you and listens.

Physical exercise. Playing sports activities acts on the mind to supply herbal chemicals that promote brilliant emotions. Physical interest moreover works on that amassed pressure and stops us from falling into horrific feelings.

Step Three: Seek Help for Difficult Emotions

Sometimes, irrespective of what movement you're taking, you genuinely can't put off mixed emotions. If you sense sad or annoying for pretty various weeks, or in case you experience very sad that you could damage your self or others, you may be missing help.

Talk to someone who will let you: a decide, a depended on character, or a therapist. For example, therapists are skilled to educate humans the manner to cope with negative emotions. They can provide you with guidelines and ideas to make you feel higher.

How to Focus on One Thing at a Time

Let me proportion with you a easy however powerful exercise, which I name: a "intellectual survey," which has the electricity to change your entire being if you allow it accompany you for your journey thru life. Are you ready for this mirrored image?

Surely you might imagine approximately several ideas, alas, you could best pick taken into consideration one among them. You will choose the most vital and relevant thoughts. That's why I name this a "mental survey," because of the fact you're looking for the maximum applicable insights.

Focus is the answer to the query above, and it could additionally be a way to reply this one: "How to find out your passion in existence." Many human beings will inform you: "Be satisfied in recent times," however it isn't always smooth. That is the electricity that intellectual surveys provide, to recognition now not best on what topics most but on what makes us happiest.

You can write all your thoughts on a single piece of paper. If five topics come to mind, write all of them down. So, ask your self, if you had to pick out such a 5 topics as the most vital one right now, what wouldn't it no longer be? The one you pick out may be your reason and your recognition from now until you attain it or it doesn't depend anymore.

Why hobby on simply one element?

Why do I need you to listing your dreams so as of significance? Quite surely, the solution is within the stamp. Because you need to hold on with the concept like a stamp on an envelope. The invitation is to understand to the concept within the mind, the body, however generally within the coronary heart.

Just like putting a stamp on an envelope until it reaches the addressee, you may keep on to one reason until you purchased the end result.

There is a Russian proverb that asserts:

"If you chase rabbits right now, you obtained't capture any. So you better pass after the pleasant you care approximately the maximum."

Why do I need you to chase high-quality one reason? So you can generate the consequences you're searching out. I want you to look returned and remember your finest successes. Pick absolutely one! I need your complete interest in this fulfillment.

You'll discover some aspect very exciting doing this: I'm certain your efforts have been focused on high-quality one trouble in which you've had superb success. Now, I am additionally happy that you aren't being very successful because of the reality your approach is virtually too huge and diffuse.

Consider this question: What is the most crucial task you need to accomplish proper now? Will doing so make it a great deal less hard so you can accomplish the opportunity responsibilities you have to do? It's approximately specializing in one purpose.

How to Tolerate Distress (Surviving a Crisis or Distressing Situation)

The conditions that people face in their each day lives should make us sense uncomfortable. The rhythm of our lifestyles is worrying and we continuously face unique adversities. It may be regular that at some point we awaken discouraged, much less excited, sadder, extra willing to cry... "despair as we recognise it." It can be regular to have a quick "melancholy" even as you're overwhelmed, but it's high-quality brief. What if this depression persists? It must make you miserable.

When time passes and you continue to enjoy sad, depressed, crying, irritating, or out of breath, you may say which you have an anxiety disease. When you're in pain, you see the entirety very darkish and gloomy, and the whole thing that happens to you is even extra terrible.

Anguish happens at the same time as a person worries excessively for no reason and motives them to lose control on an emotional degree. It could make you experience very worrying, with bodily signs and signs.

Symptoms of Anguish

Some symptoms and symptoms that stand up whilst we sense suffering are:

Chest ache

Headaches

Nervousness and shortness of breath

Palpitations

Hot flushes

Sweating

Shaking

Other possible symptoms are disappointment, reluctance, and mood swings...

Strategies to Get Out of Anguish and Be Happier

Some psychologists specialised in tension provided a few strategies to avoid or get out of pain in your existence:

Avoid anxiety and unique your feelings. Talking about what bothers you may be a remedy and a incredible help.

Make time for sports activities you enjoy and discover ways to have an excellent time. In this way, it can help you to be greater terrific and provide you with the energy to face negative conditions.

Remember a few hard situations you've got faced which have made you emotionally more potent. Every state of affairs you face has a lesson, so the lots a whole lot less time you spend failing, the earlier you can drift ahead.

Practice relaxation. Learn to breathe deeply to ease demanding moments.

Recognize that you can not manipulate the entirety. Indeed, you can not manage many stuff that arise to you, however you may manipulate the way you cope with them (how they have an effect on you). Experiencing emotions is exceptional, but permitting them to govern your existence is awful in your intellectual fitness.

Increase bodily hobby and increase healthful behavior. Through exercising, we will launch stress and relax physically and mentally.

Self-Awareness and Self-Validation (Increase Awareness and Focus on the Present Moment)

Some motives why you must recall imposing being determined for your each day existence:

There is little risk that you'll experience lifestyles a hundred%.

You have followed an subconscious way of residing with the useful resource of the use of shortcuts to get round situations that move in competition for your expectations. From proper here and now forget approximately your stuff.

You confuse what goes thru your head with truth. You are likely so absorbed to your thoughts which you pay little hobby to what is taking place outdoor of your head on your existence.

You lose recognition on what in fact subjects.

Your vision is confined. Human beings are interested in the synthetic, they best see what they decide on or how they need topics to show out. This is a component that reduces your perception of reality.

Not being there can exchange your revel in of properly-being. Do you get hold of as actual with that what scares you is actual or do you count on the catastrophic aspect of the situation? This mechanism is the primal instinct that allowed our ancestors to stay on.

Staying on autopilot is letting your emotions control you. In this enjoy, your intellectual readability is blurred. You provide all of the energy to force your moves in an emotionally reckless manner.

On the other hand, productivity suffers while the priorities of what's critical and what is much less pressing are stressed.

Mindfulness is the paintings of consciously concentrated on the present 2d without judging, as we noticed earlier. It is this kingdom of thoughts that brings your interest and recognition lower back to the winning 2d, faraway from the beyond or future. It's a skills that may be superior and practiced, and prefer some other expertise, mindfulness meditation is one of the remarkable procedures to do it. It is defined as being aware of what is taking area inside the right right here and now without judging or criticizing.

How to Be Less Critical of Yourself and Others

Self-criticism is often a form of pathological criticism, this is, it's far a terrible judgment that humans make about themselves or their movements; this idea does not assist them get the superb out of themselves. It is frequently called pathological grievance because of the reality it's miles beyond a person's manage and in the end damages their average normal performance and vanity.

Self-criticism typically takes the form of terrible comments, especially about mistakes made or goals no longer completed. More importantly, that is unconstructive complaint as it doesn't guide how we are able to use our strengths to enhance our weaknesses.

Get to Know Yourself to Tame Your Inner Voice

The first step to efficaciously deal with self-grievance is to recognize it. You have to analyze what particular subjects your critique gives with and the thoughts associated with them. It's about identifying the messages you provide your self, and in what conditions, the manner you sense and expect. You can preserve a written document so that you can examine your criticisms of your self in detail and dispassionately at a later time.

Discover the Emotions That Make You Emerge Your Critical Voice

Chapter 5: The Balance Between Two Extremes

Throughout the ebook, I honestly have talked to you about balance in emotions, the manner to stay centered, accepting what you experience, and embracing happiness and additionally disappointment, in addition to special feelings. In this final economic catastrophe, I want to speak to you about the two extremes, what's known as the "middle direction." Learn the manner to do it and what it is approximately.

What Does It Mean to "Walk the Middle Path"?

The "middle course" is a philosophy in Dialectical Behavior Therapy (DBT). In DBT, taking the middle direction approach placing stability amongst opposites. Many human beings recognized with Borderline Personality Disorder (BPD) war with excessive, painful, and overwhelming feelings, thoughts, and behaviors. It seems that many people with BPD warfare to live on or cope with life's pains in an "all-or-not something" way.

An example of this so-called "all-or-nothing" manner might be texting someone more than one times until they textual content, or conversely resisting replying to a person for a long term.

A middle route among the extremes is to deliver one or textual content messages with splendid regions and ask the opportunity man or woman to answer. Another instance might be operating so hard to satisfy a ultimate date that you feel exhausted or, conversely, now not going to the exam because of the reality the homework is without a doubt too massive. The middle course proper here is on the way to artwork, however prevent in advance than it critically damages your fitness.

I assume human beings with BPD also can discover it more hard than others to go the middle route. For someone with BPD, the feelings can be intense and the associated mind may be overwhelming. For example, someone with BPD who's ashamed can also experience emotionally fed on, nearly constantly thinking of themselves as nugatory, and may then respond to this painful emotional experience via the usage of self-harming. When I become in university, I grow to be so determined to succeed academically that I should stay up past due analyzing and now not allow myself a smash. On the other, I understand oldsters which is probably so scared of failing an examination that they're scared of analyzing.

DBT is all approximately converting patterns of emotion, belief, and conduct. It is prepared changing our problems with out judging ourselves for them. My incredible therapist informed me that to exchange how I felt, I had to exchange the manner I act. It grow to be pretty a wonder at the start. Before I changed my behavior, I needed to exchange how I felt. I felt like I didn't want to be so ashamed after I stopped self-harming. However, my therapist instructed me that the high-quality way to lessen my shame modified into to prevent performing ashamed.

Also, I assume it's simplest as soon as I experience much less worrying that I save you looking for comfort. To my marvel, I later determined out that I needed to save you looking for consolation actually so my anxiety ought to lower. I knew that searching for to assist myself backward doesn't work. These behaviors red meat up mind and feelings.

Taking the middle course has been and will continue to be important to feeling higher over the years. Instead of installing a hundred% try to burn out every day, offer your self a chunk extra area to rest and do away with blemishes. For example, whilst you deliver an e-mail, you shouldn't worry that the entirety is in capital letters or that each one the strains are perfect. The 1% of strength you store is 1% of resiliency at the end of the day.

Some examples of the center course is probably going out at the same time as you want to socialise instead of staying domestic all of the time whilst you're tired, house cleansing is a bit decrease than commonplace, or being a couple of minutes overdue for appointments on a few days. I don't assume going the center direction way you need to be precisely inside the middle, it's greater approximately being open to performing some extra or a chunk an awful lot much less than you enjoy you need to.

At first, the concept of going the center route can terrify you. Not on foot so difficult, now not punishing yourself, making mistakes, and now not spanking your self is frightening.

There are nonetheless times these days that experience very hard. However, taking the center course is how I can allow myself to reap the honour I deserve at all times, now not just once I enjoy like I've earned it.

It may be difficult to authentically validate others at the same time as you're going thru robust feelings your self. Practice self-care and know-how what you feel. Taking the middle course implies that every parties pop out in their feelings and be aware the opportunity's factor of view. When you're aware about what you've got and what you are going thru at that 2d, you will be capable of consciously go out and see the angle of the alternative.

Increase Positive Behaviors

Sometimes the most effective opportunity is the effective one. "Discover" the incredible matters a person does and praise them for that manner of being. At home you may perform a little small matters to provide once more to your own family, like placing the dishes inside the dishwasher, setting up the towels after the bathe, and placing away a few component you left untidy. As you are a teenager, recollect that your emotions are walking and on occasion they'll be stressed, it's miles normal. Make an try to do your top notch, no matter the fact that they may be small topics, you may see how to procure praise out of your dad and mom. Surely you'll encourage your self to do it later.

You can also get hold of rewards of a few kind, from information to like (first-class results). Maybe you have some more time to do some matters or a smash from nightly chores. Even pleasant time may be some issue left over to proportion with others.

Reduce Unhealthy Behaviors

Trying to change or forestall awful behavior can be one of the toughest additives of the journey. No one dreams you to act adverse, use pills, harm yourself, or come domestic after curfew. For most mother and father, the preliminary response is to enhance the punishment through penalizing the child, taking their mobile phone, or confiscating their car keys. That is at the same time as you understand that matters are awful, that you are appearing badly, but generally if there can be no emotional intelligence and information of the problem, there are not any modifications.

Experience the Natural Consequences

Natural outcomes are subjects that show up glaringly because of behavior. For example, on the identical time as you contact a heat range, you get burned; if you don't take a category, you fail; at the same time as you carelessly enjoy the motorbike, you crash. Allowing yourself to experience the natural consequences allows you to understand the impact of actions. If you don't do your homework, you're going to fail. Despite how painful it's miles to appearance it, it weighs you down but it's miles effective in gaining knowledge of that this does not help you.

Promote Value-Based Consequences

Sometimes, living those reminiscences makes the herbal consequences of what you've got had been given lived teach you. In the case of self-harm, substance abuse, and ingesting troubles (to call a few), the natural impact is more severe and I don't suggest it. When jogging at the middle route, you're comparing what is right and awful, I typically suggest which you acquire this with fee-primarily based totally without a doubt consequences in thoughts.

Everyone is imbued with values, whether or not or not they outline them or not. Shared family values may be kindness, recognize, cleanliness, protection, verbal exchange, and love.

If awful subjects happen, movements need to be taken to repair them. Of route, price-based totally absolutely consequences don't want to be reserved for immoderate instances. An regular instance is at the same time as your brother makes amusing of you due to the fact you cry or have some component. (He does now not have his values in line with this, I suggest you skip him this e-book.) You have to talk, paintings things out, and then every perform a bit problem type for the opportunity. Do your outstanding to make results instantaneous, fee-based totally totally, creative, and immediately related to the conduct you are trying to correct.

Exercises to Increase the Balance Between the Two Extremes

How to apply the middle route to have a balance?

Recognize Your Emotional State

When you are emotionally charged, the punishment or impact you pick out out is frequently extreme and vain. You also are more likely to provide in even as someone claims you, stresses you out, or has an emotional breakdown.

Sit Down with the Other Person and Get on the Same Page About the Rules and the Consequences

When you're in an emotionally suitable position, encompass the human beings involved inside the communication. Remember that rules and effects are best at the same time as they may be right now associated with the values you need to paintings on.

You can:

Tell the person who what they did harm you otherwise you didn't like it.

Listen to their factor of view, possibly it become in retaliation for a beyond act.

Apologize if applicable, and are looking for to restore matters.

Reconcile and forgive each one-of-a-type.

Start Little with the resource of Little

Pick a fantastic conduct you need to growth and discover procedures to praise it. If you need your partner to collaborate at the undertaking, you could supply a lift to it through thanking them for having participated or giving them a reward after they comply. Use this incredible reinforcement even if you have to ask them more than one times before it occurs. Real behavior change takes time.

1.   When they don't act as they need to, remind them, and allow them to recognize you're looking beforehand to them to do it.

2.   When they prevail, praise them with affirmation terms for having complied.

The abilties of going via the center path allow you to to transport inside the direction of others or to correct your self. When you discover ways to understand superb human beings's perspectives and confirm valid ones, conduct changes will become more conscious. I wish that through way of education the ones talents at domestic, relationships will enhance and adolescents might be more fun for genuinely absolutely everyone.

Sometimes the behavior of others can emerge as so immoderate which you not can cope with it for your private. If you enjoy the conduct is getting out of hand, you could talk to a supportive authority or you can lessen the space that is too deep to restore to your very very own, and take the subsequent step to help your self and others heal.

STOP: The Short Way

This is a easy and traditional mindfulness approach that strives no longer to behave automatically, so it is able to be very beneficial in your every day existence. Again, right here's a smooth mnemonic to remind you of a few steps:

The entire system may be finished as wished. You can do it in 30 seconds or 15 mins. Sometimes it's genuine to save you and see what they're telling you proper now.

Given the automated nature of our every day lives, it's far useful to set reminders of the exercise, which incorporates placing a prevent be a part of up a laptop or cellular phone show display display screen saver or writing a mnemonic somewhere.

There are many breathing techniques to reduce tension and interest at the triumphing 2nd.

A very beneficial method is to inhale for four seconds and exhale for the identical time or a bit longer (five or 6 seconds).

You must wear a watch constant to ensure you're doing it proper before you're taking hold of your hand.

Holding your breath for the same quantity of time works nicely: inhale for 4 seconds, maintain for 4 seconds, and exhale for four seconds.

By controlling the immediately of exhalation, we supply indicators to the mind that the whole thing is splendid, we lessen the interest of the alarm gadget (the sympathetic traumatic device) and set off the calming device (the parasympathetic fearful device).

If you try this for a couple of minutes, you may see that your emotional state is affected right now and you may experience calmer and with clearer thinking.

The Habit of Meditating: The Long Way

Today's worldwide is prepared to entertain us, however not continuously to live constant with our values or a clear experience of life. We are considerably excited and the information involves us from all facets: we have many social networks, new collection and films are coming out, and video video games have emerge as better and extra appealing. In addition, the idea of doing topics became famous, and it have end up the norm to sacrifice relaxation and enjoyment to advantage the excellent feasible productivity. Here, we are capable of get slowed down in all this messy information and come to be behaving like fantastic-busy automata.

If you aren't attentive, in case you do no longer take a day or in step with week to prevent and contemplate what goes on for your head, you threat dropping your freedom and succumbing to the manner of existence. Getting on the teach of inertia and automatism, killing your self little by little internal, related to feelings of emptiness, disconnecting from values and purpose, and chaining ourselves to needless pain (now not in pursuit of values and freely selected dreams), is overriding you with outdoor stimuli.

Meditation has been practiced with the useful resource of numerous cultures and religions for masses of years. This dependancy can provide you with the gap to stability the opposites thru respiratory techniques and mindfulness, therefore schooling the pursuit of an sensible thoughts, which can be finished with out buying high priced commands. While courses are constantly a terrific assist whilst exploring unknown paths, specifically inner states, cultivating meditation is close reachable and high-quality takes a hint time.

There are many strategies to exercising meditation, relying on which school you choose, but these are only a few easy tips. Maybe it works for you on the start, then you could maintain searching.

If you examine that you are in a country of peace, calm, and serenity, you could keep playing the time you need, or you can ask yourself a few questions, and the solution can simplest make certain or no. A foothold can be useful now that will help you stay focused. It permit you to refocus your interest on your breath once in a while, noticing the air getting into or from your nose; keeping your eyes on an object, a lamp or a candle; maintaining something for your hand, which encompass a photo, bracelet, or rubber ball.

Here are some examples of topics that require meditation, however you can find out questions that healthful your state of affairs:

Several subjects can appear in some unspecified time in the future of this closing step. Sometimes you'll word that there may be no clean answer and you could have a question about a question. Nothing takes place, and probably the solution is that you need to attend, you want to in reality receive the uncertainty and drift on till you've got a clearer vision of the hassle. There will also be no solutions, so you also can need to attempting to find assist or turn to someone else. Finally, a definitive solution might also additionally emerge. This happens, and it's no longer unusual at all. The hard detail is having the braveness and willingness to listen.

The solutions of a sensible thoughts have sure capabilities that cause them to smooth to distinguish from those of different minds: They are perfectly valid, nearly apparent; they relate for your values, your desires, and your private history; they may be consistent; they may be intuitive and direct so you don't need a line of reasoning to get them. They are type so they want this silence and detachment to pay attention their voices. Hence the importance of operating toward meditation.

Of direction, this received't display up each day and will require some of exercising and perseverance, however over the years it will get much less difficult after which it turns into as natural as respiration. Again, I propose that you spend as an entire lot time in meditation as possible. And it's loose! Some humans can practice for an hour a day. It may be masses initially, so I advise beginning with a couple of minutes one, , or 3 times consistent with week. But do it. This is also a brilliant opportunity to exercise the strategies that I confirmed you in the first chapters of the ebook, exactly that will help you get into the dependancy of meditating.

The closing detail may be very important because of the truth you need to combine all of the preceding content material material. Finding those middle factors in lifestyles calls for readability about our values and motive, facts a manner to encourage ourselves, expertise and regulating our emotions, and ultimately understanding how to hook up with others and experience life. In addition, we noted the want to really be given in context an almost philosophical hassle: that manage over our lives, over others, and spherical us is an illusion. We don't control some thing. At most, thru expertise and training, we will make an impact.

We want to first exert this have an effect on on ourselves, on our thoughts, emotions, and actions. Aristotle said that we can workout "political" manage over our passions. We can't strain ourselves with anger or violence. We must realise a manner to negotiate kindly. Then, when we already enjoy that we are capable of control these sources, we are able to exercise them to our relationships with others. We can effect in vicinity of manage the mind, emotions, and behavior of these round us. This possibility has a exceptional aspect and a darkish thing. By utilising this in our environment, we ought to in no manner lose sight of who we want to be and what form of relationships we want to have with others.

Chapter 6: The Four Modules Of Dbt

Mindfulness: Cultivating Present-Moment Awareness

Finding quiet moments in cutting-edge day global of constant trade and rapid pace may be difficult. True contentment inside the gift moment is rare for the reason that our minds are so regularly ate up with regrets about the past or anxieties about the destiny. But mindfulness, a sincere however effective approach, offers us with a treatment for this confused highbrow nation. We can open the door to a worldwide of clarity, presence, and nicely-being via jogging in the direction of mindfulness. This article delves into the basics of mindfulness and examines how it can decorate our physical, intellectual, and emotional fitness.

Knowing What Mindfulness Is

Fundamentally, mindfulness is the intentional, nonjudgmental exercise of listening to the modern-day 2d. It consists of purposefully focusing our hobby at the emotions, ideas, and sensations that ground in each on the spot, heading off turning into sucked into them or appearing on an impulse. Although mindfulness has its roots in antiquated contemplative traditions like Buddhism, it has turn out to be more and more popular as a mundane exercising that is open to people from all walks of lifestyles in modern day years.

The Advantages of Being Present

1. Reducing Stress: By education mindfulness, we will discover ways to step decrease again from the by no means-completing go with the glide of thoughts and issues that motive strain. Stress levels can be decreased thru making vicinity for rest and introspection with the beneficial useful resource of objectively monitoring our thoughts and emotions.

2. Increasing Mental Clarity: Mindfulness schooling improves our capability for focus and hobby. We can improve our creativity, choice-making competencies, and cognitive feature with the useful resource of teaching

our minds to be gift. It has been showed that mindfulness improves reminiscence and interest span.

3. Improving Emotional Welfare: Being aware encourages us to broaden a type and non-reactive reference to our emotions. We come to be greater emotionally resilient and experience more in control of our responses while we widely known and take shipping of our emotions. It lessens anxiety, depressive signs and symptoms, and emotional reactivity.

4. Fostering Self-Awareness: Mindfulness promotes in-depth introspection and self-getting to know. We grow to be more aware of our exercises, inclinations, and automatic reactions while we are truly gift with ourselves. This superior self-reputation offers us the potential to choose accurately and forestall assignment harmful behaviors.

5. Promoting Physical Health: Studies suggest that mindfulness training can advantage one's physical well-being. Stress reduction

techniques primarily based mostly on mindfulness had been associated with decreased blood stress, higher outstanding sleep, and a better immune tool. Mindfulness can decorate well-known nicely-being by way of manner of using lowering strain and galvanizing relaxation.

Including Mindfulness in Everyday Activities

1. Formal Practice of Meditation: Schedule a selected time frame each day to interact in mindfulness meditation. Locate a peaceful region, take a snug seat, and consciousness in your respiratory or a specific feeling. As ideas come to thoughts, well known them with kindness after which release them, bringing your interest lower lower returned to the right right here and now. As you beautify, regularly amplify your classes from shorter starts offevolved offevolved.

2. Mindful Activities: Incorporate mindfulness into everyday obligations like taking walks, ingesting, and dishwashing. Take be aware about the flavor, scent, texture, and motion

as you have interaction with the senses. Feeling grounded and comfortable can be attained thru absolutely taking element inside the ones smooth sports activities sports whilst maintaining gift-2nd popularity.

3. Mindful Breathing: Set apart a while to pay interest in your breathing on every occasion you are feeling traumatic or overburdened. Shut your eyes, take a deep breath, then launch it slowly, focusing simplest on the feeling of your breath entering and exiting your frame. This smooth exercising will let you regain your composure and popularity your thoughts.

four. Non-Judgmental Observation: Make it a exercise to check your emotions, thoughts, and physical opinions in a judgment-free way. Observe reviews as they arrive and cross in vicinity of categorizing them as appropriate or awful. This kind commentary promotes reputation and makes room for more comprehension and clarity.

By imparting get right of entry to to the richness and intensity of the triumphing 2nd, mindfulness permits us live greater sincerely and honestly. We can exchange the way we engage with the world and ourselves with the useful resource of adopting this exercise. In a way of lifestyles in which distraction and busyness are the norm, mindfulness offers a beneficial device for selling holistic well-being, reducing strain tiers, and achieving inner peace. Now, inhale deeply, input the practice of mindfulness, and find out the numerous blessings of leading a life that is completely present.

Distress Tolerance: Coping with Crisis and Urges

Distress tolerance is a concept often related to Dialectical Behavior Therapy (DBT), which have become superior through Dr. Marsha Linehan. It refers to the capability to face as a lot as and efficaciously control emotional distress, specifically sooner or later of disaster conditions or at the same time as managing extreme urges. Distress tolerance skills are critical for individuals who might also moreover moreover battle with overwhelming emotions, impulsive behaviors, or trouble handling catastrophe conditions.

Here are a few distress tolerance competencies commonly taught in DBT:

1.Self-Soothing: Engaging in sports that provide consolation and a feel of calm. This may want to in all likelihood include taking a heat bath, being attentive to soothing tune, or conducting sports sports that bring a sense of peace.

2.Distract with ACCEPTS: This acronym represents a hard and fast of distraction strategies:

Activities: Engage in sports sports that require popularity.

Contributing: Help others or interact in acts of kindness.

Comparisons: Compare your present day situation to a worse one you've got were given were given experienced or do not forget.

Emotions: Generate one among a kind feelings by way of manner of project sports that create a particular temper.

Pushing Away: Mentally set apart the trouble for a selected period.

Thoughts: Focus your mind on some thing else.

3.Self-Soothe with the 5 Senses: Use your 5 senses to interact in activities that provide comfort. This would possibly in all likelihood include searching at adorable environment, taking note of calming track, smelling exceptional scents, tasting a few element fun, or feeling the feel of a comforting object.

4.Pros and Cons List: Weigh the specialists and cons of wearing out a specific behavior. This helps human beings make more knowledgeable options in preference to acting all of a surprising.

5.Radical Acceptance: Acknowledge and take delivery of the fact of a state of affairs, although it's miles ugly. This can assist lessen emotional struggling and permit for greater effective problem-solving.

6.Turning the Mind: Make a conscious choice to just accept and tolerate the current scenario in preference to preventing closer to it. This entails deciding on to take part in the moment in area of resisting.

7.Wise Mind:

Reasonable Mind: Making alternatives primarily based totally totally on records and nicely judgment.

Emotion Mind: Making picks primarily based mostly on feelings and feelings.

Wise Mind: Combining each cause and emotion to make balanced and effective selections.

eight. Improve the Moment: Engage in sports which may be fun or offer a enjoy of success to decorate your temper and assist address misery.

It's important to observe that distress tolerance skills are just one problem of DBT. DBT additionally includes mindfulness, interpersonal effectiveness, and emotion regulation competencies. Individuals are encouraged to exercising those talents frequently, not in reality during moments of disaster, to beautify their capacity to address distressing situations through the years. If you or a person you understand is suffering with misery or urges, it is endorsed to are attempting to find professional help from a intellectual fitness professional or therapist.

Emotion Regulation: Managing Intense Feelings

Feelings are a herbal hassle of daily lifestyles. When we're stuck in traffic, we turn out to be angry. When we pass over our loved ones, we get depressed. When a person disappoints us or injures us, we may also turn out to be enraged.

Even even though we anticipate experiencing the ones feelings regularly, some human beings begin to experience greater erratic emotions. Their lives begin to be suffering from those peaks and valleys as they experience extra highs and decrease lows. People with strong emotional swings may be serene one minute and depressed or furious the subsequent.

Although anybody reports moments at the same time as their feelings spiral out of manipulate, a few humans revel in this on a everyday basis. They may additionally moreover say and do topics they later regret due to their speedy shifting emotions. They ought to possibly jeopardize their credibility or bitter relationships.

A person also can end up emotionally uncontrollable for quite a few motives. They might be more vulnerable to the ones brief changes due to genetics. They won't have discovered out the talents or visible notable fashions of emotional regulation. When they come upon sports that remind them of ugly reviews from the beyond, they may lose manipulate. Physical changes like fatigue or a drop in blood sugar can also make a person lose control of their emotions.

Whatever the reason of our emotional instability, we are capable of enhance our self-law abilties, which is ideal news. Learning the way to manipulate our feelings is something that would assist each person. The capability to more effectively manipulate our feelings is called emotional law.

What do emotional regulation and control advocate?

Any movement that modifies the depth of an emotional experience falls beneath the class of emotional manipulate and regulation. It does no longer advocate repressing or evading feelings. You have manage over the feelings you revel in and the manner you express them when you have emotional regulation abilties.

In the prevent, it all comes right proper down to having the potential to correctly modify our feelings the usage of quite a few techniques.

A man or woman's ability to control their feelings varies from character to character. They have a excessive emotional intelligence and are aware of their private emotions as well as the ones of others. Despite the impact that they'll be definitely "glaringly calm," the ones humans additionally sense lousy every now and then. They've handiest currently received coping mechanisms that permit them manipulate hard emotions.

Fortunately, emotional self-law is a dynamic amazing. It is viable to accumulate and extend emotional regulation talents over the years. Your bodily and intellectual nicely-being can every advantage from studying a manner to deal with unsightly activities.

Why is emotional control crucial?

It is expected human beings as adults to control our emotions in a way that each advantages society and allows us to get by way of manner of manner of in existence. Problems can stand up whilst our feelings take manage human beings.

Emotional regulation can be hampered through numerous topics. These embody our perceptions of unsightly feelings or our incapacity to manipulate our feelings. Stressful activities can sometimes elicit especially sturdy emotions.

The effect emotional instability may additionally have on our interpersonal relationships is one way it may damage us. For example, we're willing to mention hurtful topics to people spherical us and cause them to distance themselves at the same time as we're unable to control our anger. We might probable need to spend time mending relationships or remorse the topics we've got said.

Not only can an loss of capability to control our emotions damage our relationships, but it could moreover cause us damage in my view. Overwhelming depression can lessen well-being and result in useless suffering. Unrelenting fear can prevent us from taking possibilities and experiencing new topics in lifestyles.

five strategies you must learn how to manipulate your emotions

We can research numerous strategies to govern our feelings.

1. Make room.

Emotions come on speedy. Instead of questioning, "Now I can be irritated," we simply get tight-lipped and enraged all of a sudden. So pausing is the first-rate gift we are able to supply ourselves close to handling difficult feelings. Inhaled deeply. Reduce the rate at which the motive and response get up.

2. Being aware of your feelings

Being capable of understand your emotions is a capacity that is without a doubt as crucial. The practices that Dr. Judson Brewer, MD, Ph.D. Indicates will let you turn out to be greater inquisitive about your very own bodily reactions. Pay hobby to your self and ask your self, wherein for your body are you feeling matters? Are you feeling nauseous? Is your pulse pounding? Do you have got headache or neck anxiety?

Your physical signs can be signs of your emotional us of a. Asking questions about your bodily state also can divert your interest and decrease the depth of the sensation.

three. Labeling your emotions

The capability to call your emotions assist you to regain manipulate over your times after you have got were given observed them. What time period should you operate to give an explanation for the emotions you're experiencing? Is it resentment, unhappiness, anger, or unhappiness? What is it, over again?

Fear is one powerful feeling that often lurks under others.

It's commonplace for us to experience multiple emotions simultaneously, so do not be afraid to call any feelings you may be experiencing. Next, delve a hint in addition. What are you terrified of, if you are afraid? If you're indignant, what or whom are you indignant with? Gaining the functionality to choose out out your emotions will convey you one step in the direction of expressing them to different people.

4. Embracing the feeling

It is regular and herbal for us to react to situations with feelings. Acknowledge that your emotions of anger or worry are valid as opposed to punishing your self for them. Make an try and be type to yourself and increase grace to your self. Acknowledge that feeling emotions is a mean human response.

five. Making mindfulness a dependancy

Being aware includes being aware of our inner selves, which permits us to "live inside the 2nd." Make nonjudgmental observations about what is going on spherical you thru the use of your senses. These talents allow you to in maintaining composure and stopping destructive concept patterns while experiencing emotional distress.

Seven strategies that will help you control your feelings

People can increase numerous emotion law strategies to reinforce their coping mechanisms. It's essential to evaluate which techniques are only and which ones to steer easy of.

Two important training can be used to explain emotional regulation. The first is reappraisal, which involves changing our mind-set on a situation an brilliant manner to modify our response. Suppression is the second, and it's miles related to greater negative effects. Studies display screen that suppressing our emotions is established to sadness and coffee nicely-being.

Let's look at seven strategies for tremendous and healthful emotion manipulate.

1. Determine and reduce stressors

It isn't always virtually beneficial to try and suppress or be afraid of terrible emotions. However, you furthermore may moreover do not want to constantly place your self in uncomfortable conditions. When you begin to enjoy strong feelings, start watching any styles or contributing factors. Honesty and curiosity are wanted for this. Did you experience a feel of smallness? Strong feelings, in particular those we hold hidden, frequently rise up from our ingrained fears. What goes on to your immediate environment, and what recollections does it reason for you?

Once you have got decided which triggers they'll be, you could inspect why they're so critical and whether you could lessen their have an impact on. For instance, a CEO who struggled in math elegance might be embarrassed to confess that he receives angry even as speaking about numbers. Maybe understanding this trigger is enough. Alternatively, the CEO may moreover decide to see a personal preview of the monthly charts as a way to save you feeling as even though he is being not on time thru virtually anybody else.

2. Pay interest to physical courtroom instances

Be aware about your feelings, especially whether or not or no longer or now not you experience fatigued or hungry. These elements may also moreover intensify your feelings and lead you to interpret them greater strongly. You can alter your emotional reaction if you may cope with the underlying hassle (along facet hunger or tiredness).

3. Think approximately the narrative you're telling yourself.

When records is missing, we provide our private details to fill within the gaps. If you haven't heard from a member of the family in a while, you might be feeling rejected and wondering they don't care approximately you anymore.

Consider your options earlier than assigning blame. What extraordinary elements might probably exist? What else is probably occurring with the member of the family in the example that could prevent them from contacting you? Might they be sick or preoccupied? Do they've got suitable intentions however a addiction of forgetting to hold their word?

Add "similar to me" on the cease, regardless of the other character's motivation or path of motion (there may be nearly constantly some other man or woman worried). It serves as a useful reminder that they are moreover fallible people.

four. Use positive self-communicate

We can also begin telling ourselves things like, "I messed up again," or "every body else is so lousy," while our feelings get too much for us to deal with. Positive remarks can take the location of a number of this terrible self-talk if you deal with your self with empathy. Sayings like "I usually try so tough" or "People are doing the quality they are capable of" will will let you revel in higher about yourself. This change can also furthermore reduce the depth of our emotions. You no longer need to area blame or extrapolate the problem past the context for you to precise your frustration with a scenario that isn't operating.

5. Select your path of movement.

Most of the time, we can pick out our direction of motion. You probably understand how your relationships are suffering if you regularly react to irritated emotions via snapping at people. It's possible that you can additionally observe that it hurts. Alternatively, although it feels appropriate proper now, the prolonged-term consequences damage.

Remember which you have the energy to decide the manner you want to react the subsequent time you enjoy worry or anger. That acknowledgment has incredible electricity. Maybe you need to attempt responding in a one-of-a-kind way in place of lash out? Is it viable that allows you to specific your anger to someone with out using harsh language? Become inquisitive about the consequences of changing your solutions. What end up your feeling? What became the opportunity character's response?

6. Seek out glad emotions

It is in our nature to provide horrible emotions more weight than extraordinary ones. We call this negativity bias. Emotions which can be awful, such as disgust, anger, and unhappiness, often have a immoderate emotional weight. Contentment, curiosity, and thankfulness are quieter feelings. Developing the workout of recognizing the ones pinnacle matters can increase resilience and popular well being.

7. Look for a counselor

Controlling our private emotions is not usually smooth. A immoderate degree of self-attention is vital. We begin to lose our capability to govern our emotions even as we're going via a tough duration. We occasionally require a companion, which embody a therapist, to help us in growing stronger self-law abilities. Thankfully, there are hundreds of recuperation techniques that would teach us the manner to control our emotions greater correctly.

Emotional regulation sickness: what's it?

A person with emotional regulation disorder struggles to control their feelings. Dysregulation is the time period used to provide an reason behind this inadequate emotional law. The lack of capability to manipulate one's emotions or maintain reactions inner an less luxurious sure is referred to as dysregulation.

Dramatic mood swings are much more likely to arise in someone with emotional law disorder. These versions then have a terrible impact at the person's behavior.

A illness of emotional regulation may additionally furthermore reason some of the following symptoms:

Having hassle establishing and keeping healthy relationships

Acts of self-destruction

Excessive sensitivity

Frequently having tantrums or meltdowns

Emotional outbursts directed at a person who did no longer cause the harm

Other mental fitness conditions also can coexist with emotional law disease. Emotional law is often made greater difficult with the useful resource of using issues like borderline individual illness, melancholy, or strain.

Interpersonal Effectiveness: Building Healthy Relationships

The status quo and protection of healthy relationships is the intention of DBT's interpersonal effectiveness competencies. Those who've lived prolonged, high-quality lives in healthful relationships regularly personal the ones competencies really. These tendencies had been broken down by means of the usage of way of DBT and converted into four top notch skills. Everyone can benefit from mastering those techniques, but people who be concerned thru attachment troubles or have skilled trauma will advantage most.

THINK

The extra current-day DBT interpersonal effectiveness talent is THINK. It become created to reduce animosity inside the direction of awesome humans. Although you could now not constantly want to use this skill, it's going to are available in to be had whilst you're having hassle with others and you feel down.

Consider the conditions from the point of view of the alternative individual. Is she also furious? Do you observed you are unreasonable, and she or he or he thinks you are unreasonable?

Demonstrate empathy via asking your self how the alternative character can also feel. Give yourself a second to enjoy her feelings.

Interpretations: of the movements of the alternative individual. Consider capacity causes for her actions that irritated you. To assist you live open-minded, start with ludicrous justifications earlier than transferring straight away to extra realistic ones.

"She works for the lab and is doing exams on how suggest she may be and get away with it. She wasn't raised inside the lab, but she grow to be raised in a lab and would not have a heart. Her hamster exceeded away this morning, and he or she or he is the usage of meanness to cover her grief → She battles melancholy and lately had a meltdown that triggered her being unsightly. As a human, she have end up irritated and did not manipulate it nicely. Everybody makes mistakes.

Hopefully, after finishing those first 3 steps, you could feel less irritated and be able to anticipate and act greater rationally. That will help you inside the next steps.

Observe the opportunity man or woman: Observe her attempts to be thoughtful and beautify the bond among them. Even despite the fact that you assumed she grow to be angry, you can see that she seems afraid. Even no matter the truth that you may not be friends sincerely however, you must have noticed that she smiled at you. Just be aware of it; there can be not anything you need to do approximately it proper now.

Generosity to your answer: This does no longer require you to miss and forgive right away. This absolutely shows that you speak with kindness. "I want we can healing this within the future. What you said to me harm." might be your response. I want a few region proper now. In the long term, a well mannered respond is probably more beneficial to the relationship than shouting and name-calling.

One may also want to classify the acronym THINK as an interpersonal distress tolerance expertise. The following interpersonal effectiveness techniques might be clean at the way to take a look at once you're in a feature in which you experience able to controlling your feelings toward the alternative individual.

FAST

FAST focuses on preserving your dignity in the face of struggle of words. Prior to the usage of them , you should use them sequentially.

Fair: Both to others and to yourself. This encompasses your thoughts further for your conduct. "I'm powerless in this case" or "They're the worst!" are examples of dramatic or judgmental mind or statements which you do no longer use whilst you're being fair. As an possibility, you is probably thinking a few component like, "What's taking place for that individual, and what is taking region for me?" or "What were the elements of truth, notwithstanding the reality that I did not agree with most of what he absolutely said?"

No: Sorry may not suggest you want to by no means make an apology; in fact, apologizing has a quite powerful impact on relationships. But while you have not finished something incorrect, you do no longer should make an apology.

Maintain your morals: Take a stance on your beliefs. If you're uncertain of your beliefs, check your self to discover what your values are. Tell the truth approximately your values. You cannot actually price family if you declare to price them however actively avoid them. You may also want to put in writing your modern values as well as your ideal values for the future.

Sincere: Be honest with every your self and other humans. Are you making topics worse than they may be? Do you downplay it? Are you being honest?

Regardless of techniques you feel approximately the end end result, you could maintain your composure and leave a scenario feeling fantastic about your self via using the usage of following the four steps of FAST.

Though they'll be finished to all types of interpersonal communication, THINK and FAST are mainly beneficial in conflictual situations. You can amplify an exceptional courting via normal interpersonal communication thru the usage of the strategies GIVE and DEAR MAN.

GIVE

In any sort of interpersonal interplay, the GIVE expertise is beneficial. Regardless of the duration of time you've got been married or met this person, GIVE will aid the improvement and safety of wholesome relationships.

Gentle in your way: Being gentle method that you are considerate of the emotions of the alternative man or woman. By doing this, you can make the alternative individual revel in greater cherished and much much less attacked throughout your communique. When there is no defensiveness, communication is constantly extra effective.

Curious approximately what the opportunity person has to mention: Expressions of hobby may be expressed verbally or nonverbally. You can use phrases to probe the individual with inquiries approximately her statements or to elicit easy "huh" or "oh in reality?" reactions. Making a facial functions, maintaining eye contact, and being attentive to what is being said are all techniques to reveal hobby via body language.

Validate: By reflecting yet again to the alternative character the feelings you are experiencing, you may display to her that you have heard and understood what she is pronouncing. You can also respond, "How irritating! "if she tells you that her buddy has canceled their lunch date for the 1/3 time in a row. You should be in reality disenchanted!

Easy manner: Throughout the verbal exchange, assignment a experience of ease and luxury. You'll encounter as extra quality.

For the GIVE information for use, communication must be each verbal and nonverbal. You'll be higher organized to speak with humans in all your relationships in case you take the ones steps.

DEAR MAN

The interpersonal capacity known as "DEAR MAN" is the capability to in a well mannered way and efficaciously make requests so you can set up and keep a dating, no matter whether or not or no longer you emerge as getting what you want.

Give a brief description of the situations: Saying some trouble like "My friends are going to look the fashionable comic ebook film this weekend" can succinctly sum up your plans to visit the movies in conjunction with your buddies.

Tell humans what you want: "I'd want to accompany them to the movies."

In a well mannered, non-aggressive manner, state why this is important to you. "It might be sincerely huge if I may additionally need to spend time with them due to the truth I have now not been able to thinking about that song season commenced out."

When you do get preserve of what you requested, reinforce: "I swear, in advance than I head out to the movie, my room may be spotless and my homework finished."

Be aware and continue to be in the present. Don't pressure about the past or the future, or about what people will keep in mind you in case you are not able to wait. Simply stay in that at once.

Look Assured: Are you alternatively afraid to ask your boss for a boost? That's no longer crucial for her to understand. Be first-rate to method the problem with warranty.

When it does no longer seem like you will get the very last results you've got been hoping for, negotiate and display a few flexibility. Find a together agreeable middle ground with the aid of negotiating.

Many teenagers make desires, ask incoherently, or do no longer ask in any respect in preference of getting what they need as opposed to asking for what they want.

Not quality can interpersonal effectiveness skills gain human beings managing attachment issues and borderline individual disease, however they also can gain all of us in search of to improve their relationships with others.

Chapter 7: Skills Training And Practical Exercises

Larning and Applying Mindfulness Techniques

Mindfulness is a practice that includes bringing one's interest to the prevailing second. It has its roots in historical contemplative traditions, especially in Buddhism, however in present day-day years, it has received big recognition as an earthly exercise with severa intellectual and bodily fitness benefits. Learning and making use of mindfulness strategies can be transformative for humans in managing stress, improving awareness, and improving regular nicely-being.

Learning Mindfulness Techniques:

Start with the Basics:

Begin with easy mindfulness sports. Focus in your breath, sensations on your body, or the sounds spherical you.

Mindful respiratory is a common location to begin. Pay interest in your breath, the upward thrust and fall of your chest or the feeling of air passing via your nostrils.

Guided Meditations:

Use guided meditations led by way of way of skilled teachers. Many belongings, collectively with apps and online platforms, offer guided education to assist novices establish a recurring.

Mindful Observation:

Engage in aware commentary of your environment. Take look at of colours, shapes, and details. This allows anchor your hobby in the gift moment.

Body Scan:

Practice a frame test meditation, in which you systematically supply interest to every a part of your frame. This permits in developing frame attention and relaxation.

Non-judgmental Awareness:

Cultivate non-judgmental attention of your mind and emotions. Instead of labeling them as right or horrible, in fact have a look at and renowned them without attachment.

Applying Mindfulness Techniques:

In Daily Activities:

Bring mindfulness into each day sporting events. Whether it is consuming, taking walks, or washing dishes, reputation on the hobby reachable in preference to letting your mind wander.

Mindful Breathing in Stressful Situations:

When faced with stress, workout conscious respiratory. Take a few deep breaths, that specialize in every inhale and exhale. This can help alter emotions and decrease the effect of stressors.

Mindful Listening:

Practice aware listening in conversations. Truly pay attention to what others are saying without mentally making ready your response. This improves conversation and empathy.

Mindful Work:

Apply mindfulness at work. Take brief breaks to reputation on your breath or engage in quick mindfulness physical activities to enhance attention and decrease workplace stress.

Mindful Walking:

Incorporate aware strolling into your habitual. Pay hobby to the sensation of every step, the movement of your body, and the environment round you.

Mindfulness Apps:

Use mindfulness apps that offer reminders and guided lessons. These will can help you integrate mindfulness into your each day existence and offer guide in growing a normal exercising.

Challenges and Tips:

Consistency is Key:

Like any knowledge, mindfulness calls for ordinary exercise. Set apart devoted time each day to your mindfulness workout.

Patience and Non-Judgment:

Be affected person with yourself. It's herbal for the mind to wander. When it takes location, lightly deliver your recognition again to the prevailing with out judgment.

Adapt to Preferences:

Explore awesome mindfulness strategies and find what works super for you. Some people may also determine on sitting meditation, at the identical time as others discover mindfulness in motion (e.G., yoga) extra powerful.

Community Support:

Joining a mindfulness institution or network can offer help and motivation. Sharing evaluations and insights with others can enhance your mindfulness adventure.

Incorporating mindfulness into your lifestyles is a private and ongoing method. It's no longer about accomplishing a selected united states however as an alternative approximately cultivating reputation and presence in every second. As you still exercise, you can locate that mindfulness will become a treasured device for dealing with pressure, improving attention, and fostering substantial well-being.

Developing Distress Tolerance Strategies

The capability to tolerate pain is vital for coping with difficult and frightening times. People can higher manipulate stress, trouble, and emotional discomfort through the use of studying the way to tolerate ache. These strategies are often a mainstay of dialectical behavior remedy (DBT), a recuperation modality that places a robust emphasis on developing emotional law capabilities. The following are some important factors and techniques for increasing misery tolerance:

Comprehending Distress Tolerance

Acknowledging Reality:

Recognize and are available to phrases with the fact that suffering exists. Denying or keeping off scary instances can often make the trouble worse. The first step toward effective distress tolerance is recognition.

Crisis versus distress:

Differentiate between a catastrophe and misery. Distress isn't always usually snug, but a disaster calls for brief response. Making the right coping approach options is aided via information the versions.

Techniques for Tolerating Distress:

Being aware:

To keep your experience of gift-2d hobby, engage in mindfulness. To assemble a intellectual place which can withstand pain, strive education aware breathing and nonjudgmental concept assertion.

Self-Relieving Tasks:

Take thing in relaxing and cushty activities. This can entail spending time in nature, having a warmth tub, or listening to relaxing track.

Strategies for Diversion:

Turn your interest away from frightening mind or events for a short whilst. To take a mental excursion, this may entail analyzing a ebook, searching a film, or taking on a interest.

Skills to Survive a Crisis:

Learn specialised crisis control techniques, together with assembling a disaster survival bundle with items and sports activities that provide solace and diversion.

Wise thoughts:

Develop the functionality to get proper of get entry to on your "smart mind," that could be a mind that balances reason and emotion. This consists of the utilization of each reason and emotion to inform options.

TIPP Skills:

Quickly decreasing emotional arousal may be accomplished by way of using using using strategies like temperature, excessive workout, paced respiration, and matched muscle rest (TIPP). Doing complete of lifestyles exercise or sprinkling cold water for your face, as an example, can right away calm you down.

Radical Acknowledgment:

Accept with radicalism that there are topics in existence which might be from your control. Although it does not endorse you need to don't forget the situations, accepting them can reduce emotional pain.

List of Pros and Cons:

Make a list of the benefits and drawbacks of giving in for your impulses. This aids in weighing the feasible consequences and permitting extra knowledgeable choice-making.

Gratitude in Self-Talk:

Use self-talk this is uplifting and maintaining to fight awful mind. Swap out catastrophic wondering for additonal realistic and balanced viewpoints.

Advice for Acquiring a Distress-Tolerance

Continual Application:

Distress tolerance gets higher with exercise, similar to a few different know-how. Even whilst there is not a catastrophe, exercise misery tolerance carrying activities on a regular basis to strengthen the abilities.

Create a Toolbox:

Assemble a toolkit containing exceptional strategies to address strain. Not each tactic is powerful in each circumstance, so flexibility is made possible by the use of approach of having quite a number of system.

Consult a Professional:

If you're struggling to create and workout misery tolerance techniques for your private, recollect getting help from a highbrow health expert.

Think and Grow:

After applying techniques for distress tolerance, hold in thoughts what went well and what did not. By reflecting on yourself, you may enhance the way you control situations inside the future.

Include Others Who Can Help:

Talk about your dreams for misery tolerance with pals or family who may be encouraging. Support networks can provide obligation and motivation.

Recall that everybody's journey is one-of-a-kind and that misery tolerance is a skills that can be superior over time.

You can provide a lift to your resilience and decorate your capacity to cope with difficult conditions through adopting those strategies into your normal existence and frequently the usage of them. If you're having problem setting the ones techniques into workout in your very very own, consulting a highbrow fitness professional can provide you individualized help and help.

Mastering Emotion Regulation Skills

Maintaining highbrow fitness and controlling one's emotional reactions to 1 in each of a kind times require the capacity to alter feelings. Acquiring those skills consists of comprehending, embracing, and regulating feelings in a way that fosters bendy conduct and highbrow properly-being. The following are critical factors and strategies for growing emotion regulation talents:

Comprehending Emotion Management

Emotional Consciousness:

Accurately apprehend and label the emotions you're experiencing. Effective emotion law is built in this self-attention.

Distinguishing Between Emotions:

Acknowledge the subtle distinctions amongst brilliant emotions. Knowing whether or now not or not you're experiencing delight, unhappiness, tension, or anger lets in you to apply extra centered regulation strategies.

The Mind-Body Link:

Keep a be careful for the bodily manifestations of diverse emotions. Comprehending the physiological expression of feelings can provide supplementary indicators for self-law.

Strategies for Regulating Emotions

Cognitive Evaluation:

Modify your mind-set on a situation to have an effect on your emotional response. This consists of rephrasing mind to offer a extra exquisite or balanced point of view.

Acceptance and Mindfulness:

By being aware, you may check and take transport of your emotions without passing judgment. This involves dwelling in the present and letting emotions come and skip without allowing them to manipulate you.

Techniques for Deep Breathing and Relaxation:

Practice current muscle rest and deep respiratory strategies to assuage your frame's physiological response to pressure and intense feelings.

Write with Expression:

Processing and regulating your feelings may be aided thru retaining a magazine of your feelings and critiques. Write about your feelings, reading the underlying thoughts and ideals, along element the reasons in the returned of them.

Activation of Behavior:

Take difficulty in topics that make you experience happy or carried out. Emotions and mood can gain from effective behaviors.

Effectiveness of Interactions:

Learn how to speak successfully so you can assertively precise your desires and feelings. Emotional distress can be reduced and misunderstandings can be prevented with smooth verbal exchange.

Establish a Secure Area:

Choose an area, both intellectual or physical, wherein you may circulate on the equal time as you are feeling crushed. This is probably a peaceful room, a nicely-preferred outdoor location, or simplest a protection-inducing visualization exercising.

Establish Limits:

Healthy obstacles should be set up and communicated on your relationships. By being aware of and open about your limitations, you can avoid emotional overload.

Ask for Social Assistance:

Discuss your emotions with a therapist, member of the family, or relied on buddy. Social guide can offer mindset, empathy, and validation.

Suggestions for Developing Emotional Control

Exercise Frequently:

Practice makes ideal as regards to the skills of emotion law. Participate in everyday physical activities and techniques to strengthen and bolster your talents.

Consider the Patterns:

Consider any recurrent subjects on your emotional reactions. Targeted intervention is possible while triggers and ordinary reactions are understood.

Create a Toolbox:

Create a custom designed toolkit with the methods which is probably pleasant for you. Being adaptable in numerous situations is made feasible through the utilization of having a numerous set of gear.

Self-Restraint:

Have empathy for your self. Recognize that pretty a few emotions are felt with the beneficial aid of absolutely everyone and that it is appropriate to accomplish that. You must be kind to your self as you may a pal.

Take Advice from Experience

After resolving tough emotional situations, hold in thoughts what went nicely and what failed to. Make use of those observations to improve your approach going in advance.

Consult a Professional:

Seeking the recommendation of a intellectual health professional is a few component you want to think about in case you're having trouble mastering the way to govern your emotions. They are able to provide tailor-made advice and methods.

Being capable of control your emotions is a non-prevent device that calls for exercise, self-focus, and a self-discipline to non-public improvement. Through the each day software program of these techniques and ordinary practice, you could improve your capability for effective emotion regulation, at the manner to enhance your intellectual and emotional health.

Enhancing Interpersonal Effectiveness

Enhancing interpersonal effectiveness includes developing and refining competencies that make contributions to splendid and effective interactions with others. Effective interpersonal abilties are critical for constructing healthy relationships, every for my part and professionally. Here are key factors and strategies for enhancing interpersonal effectiveness:

Key Components of Interpersonal Effectiveness

Communication Skills:

Develop clear and assertive verbal exchange. Express your thoughts, feelings, and desires brazenly on the same time as respecting the perspectives of others.

Practice lively being attentive to actually apprehend what others are speaking. This consists of giving your whole interest, asking clarifying questions, and paraphrasing to ensure expertise.

Empathy:

Cultivate empathy by manner of putting your self in others' shoes. Understand and validate their emotions and perspectives, even in case you do now not agree. Empathy fosters connection and mutual records.

Conflict Resolution:

Learn powerful war decision abilities. Address conflicts lightly and constructively, focusing on finding answers in region of placing blame.

Use "I" statements to precise the way you enjoy and what you need, that could assist reduce defensiveness in others.

Setting Boundaries:

Establish and talk easy boundaries in your relationships. This includes knowledge your limits and expressing them assertively to maintain a wholesome stability.

Non-Verbal Communication:

Be aware of your frame language, facial expressions, and gestures. Non-verbal cues can carry as an entire lot, if no longer greater, information than terms.

Adaptability:

Be bendy and adaptable for your conversation fashion. Adjust your technique based completely on the desires and possibilities of the individuals or agencies you're interacting with.

Social Awareness:

Develop social attention with the aid of the usage of being attuned to social cues and dynamics. Understand the emotional tone of a situation and regulate your conduct consequently.

Interpersonal Effectiveness Strategies:

DEARMAN:

Use the DEARMAN acronym (Describe, Express, Assert, Reinforce, Stay Mindful, Appear Confident) from Dialectical Behavior Therapy (DBT) to efficaciously assert yourself in interpersonal situations.

GIVE:

Employ the GIVE acronym (Gentle, Interested, Validate, Easy Manner) to enhance your capability to be assertive while maintaining first-rate relationships.

Clarify Expectations:

Clearly communicate expectancies in relationships and collaborative efforts. This consists of expressing your expectations and information the expectancies of others.

Positive Feedback:

Provide pleasant and positive comments. Acknowledge others for his or her strengths and contributions, and offer comments in a way that promotes boom and development.

Apologize Effectively:

Learn to apologize sincerely and take duty on your movements. A actual apology consists of acknowledging the impact of your behavior and expressing a determination to best change.

Cultural Sensitivity:

Be culturally sensitive and privy to variety for your interactions. Respect and appreciate variations in cultural backgrounds, perspectives, and communication patterns.

Tips for Enhancing Interpersonal Effectiveness:

Self-Reflection:

Regularly mirror in your interpersonal interactions. Consider what went well and regions for improvement. Self-consciousness is the foundation for increase.

Continuous Learning:

Be open to gaining knowledge of and enhancing your interpersonal competencies constantly. Seek feedback from others and actively paintings on addressing areas of challenge.

Chapter 8: The Role Of Dialectics In Dbt

Understanding Dialectical Thinking

In DBT, the time period "dialectical" refers to the synthesis of opposites.

Here are a few key additives of statistics dialectical questioning in DBT:

Synthesis of Opposites: Dialectical Thinking involves accepting and integrating opposing viewpoints or apparent contradictions. It encourages human beings to recognize the validity of diverse perspectives and discover a center floor.

Dialectical Dilemmas: Individuals regularly enjoy internal conflicts or dilemmas. These are situations in which seemingly opposite things can every be right. For example, a person may in all likelihood enjoy each the need for independence and the preference for connection. DBT enables people navigate the ones dilemmas and discover a balance.

Validation and Change: DBT emphasizes the importance of validating a person's experience at the same time as moreover encouraging exchange. Validating manner acknowledging and accepting the character's emotions and thoughts, even though they seem contradictory. At the equal time, the treatment promotes exchange via the use of using helping human beings enlarge talents to manipulate their emotions and behaviors efficiently.

Acceptance and Commitment: Dialectical Thinking includes the concept of radical recognition. This includes really accepting the modern-day scenario, although it's painful or tough, at the equal time as additionally spotting the want for alternate. The aim is to find a balance among popularity and dedication to personal boom and outstanding trade.

Dialectical Behavior Therapy (DBT) Skills: DBT consists of specific competencies schooling modules, and those competencies are designed to assist human beings boom a more dialectical approach to wondering and behaving. For example, misery tolerance abilities help people address difficult emotions, at the equal time as emotion regulation talents popularity on expertise and coping with severe feelings.

Balancing Caring for Self and Others: Dialectical Thinking in DBT encourages people to find out a balance amongst stressful for themselves and thinking about the wishes of others. This is critical for building and maintaining healthy relationships.

Nonjudgmental Stance: Practicing a nonjudgmental stance is essential in DBT. It involves drawing near mind, emotions, and behaviors without harsh judgment. This nonjudgmental angle fosters a extra open and receptive attitude.

By incorporating dialectical questioning, DBT interests to help human beings triumph over rigid, black-and-white wondering patterns, lessen impulsive behaviors, and broaden greater adaptive techniques of handling emotions and interpersonal traumatic situations. It is particularly powerful for humans struggling with emotion dysregulation, self-damage, and dating problems.

Balancing Acceptance and Change

The technique emphasizes locating a synthesis among accepting the prevailing fact and committing to creating effective adjustments. Here's an exploration of the way this balance is completed:

Dialectical Abstinence: DBT encourages a stability among accepting wherein a person is in the period in-between and committing to alternate. This is regularly known as "dialectical abstinence." It approach that even as human beings work closer to changing dangerous behaviors, they get hold of that, inside the short time period, entire abstinence may be hard. This popularity can reduce the shame and guilt related to setbacks, fostering a extra compassionate and practical thoughts-set.

Radical Acceptance: A key concept in DBT is radical reputation, which includes absolutely acknowledging and embracing the truth of the contemporary state of affairs without judgment. It might not advocate approving or liking the scenario; rather, it is about accepting what is. This popularity is a important basis for change, because it lets in people to transport in advance without being weighed down via resistance or denial.

Validation: Validation is an important problem of DBT. Therapists work to validate the character's emotions, thoughts, and stories, reinforcing the concept that their reactions are understandable given their specific occasions. Validating feelings creates an surroundings of understanding and splendor, selling a enjoy of self-worth.

Behavioral Change Strategies: While accepting the modern-day america is critical, DBT is likewise motion-oriented. It presents particular behavioral trade techniques to assist people amplify extra healthy coping mechanisms, improve emotional regulation, and decorate interpersonal abilities. This determination to exchange is essential to the restoration gadget.

Mindfulness: Mindfulness is a middle element of DBT and plays a important feature in balancing popularity and trade. Mindfulness consists of taking note of the prevailing second without judgment. By cultivating mindfulness, people could have a have a look at their mind and emotions without getting entangled in them, selling both beauty and exchange.

Dialectical Strategies: Therapists in DBT often use dialectical techniques to assist people navigate reputedly conflicting dreams. For example, finding a balance among accepting oneself as they will be even as additionally acknowledging the need for non-public boom. These techniques promote flexibility in wondering and behavior.

Commitment to Therapy: Engaging in DBT calls for a dedication to the recuperation method. This willpower is composed of every accepting the challenges of the existing and actively strolling toward change. The recovery dating itself embodies the dialectic of popularity and exchange, presenting a supportive and validating environment for increase.

The stability among elegance and change in DBT isn't a static kingdom however a dynamic technique. Individuals bypass thru levels of recognition and determination, steadily constructing a extra resilient and skillful method to existence's challenges. This synthesis of reputation and change is at the coronary coronary heart of DBT's effectiveness in helping people create a lifestyles without a doubt well worth living.

Chapter 9: Integrating Dbt Into Everyday Life

Incorporating DBT Principles into Relationships and Work

Incorporating Dialectical Behavior Therapy (DBT) concepts into relationships and paintings environments can motive advanced conversation, collaboration, and widespread nicely-being. Here's how DBT thoughts may be accomplished in the ones contexts:

Relationships:

Mindful Communication:

DBT Principle: Mindfulness is important in DBT, and it could beautify communique via manner of selling active listening and non-judgmental consciousness.

Application: Practice being sincerely determined in conversations. Listen actively without interrupting, and reply mindfully in preference to reactively. This fosters facts and connection.

Emotional Regulation:

DBT Principle: Recognize and manage extreme feelings without impulsive reactions.

Application: In conflicts, take a moment to apprehend and validate your emotions. Communicate your emotions assertively and constructively, keeping off blame or complaint. Encourage your partner to specific themselves further.

Interpersonal Effectiveness:

DBT Principle: Learn effective communique capabilities and assertiveness to navigate relationships.

Application: Clearly precise your goals, set barriers, and negotiate compromises on the equal time as crucial. Use "DEAR MAN" (Describe, Express, Assert, Reinforce, Mindful, Appear assured, Negotiate) competencies to speak greater efficiently.

Validation:

DBT Principle: Validate your non-public and others' critiques and feelings.

Application: Practice acknowledging and validating your companion's feelings, however the fact that you could now not without a doubt apprehend them. This fosters a supportive environment and strengthens the emotional connection in the relationship.

Wise Mind in Decision-Making:

DBT Principle: Integrate emotional and rational wondering to make balanced choices.

Application: When making selections collectively, recall each emotional and logical components. Strive for a "clever mind" technique that aligns with shared values and lengthy-time period dreams, minimizing impulsive reactions.

Work:

Mindful Work Practices:

DBT Principle: Mindfulness can reduce stress and decorate interest.

Application: Incorporate mindfulness practices into your paintings regular. Take short breaks for mindful respiration, exercise staying actually engaged in responsibilities, and method worrying situations with a non-judgmental mind-set.

Emotional Regulation inside the Workplace:

DBT Principle: Manage emotions successfully to prevent impulsive reactions.

Application: When confronted with stressors at paintings, take a second to pick out out and regulate your feelings. Avoid impulsive responses and do not forget splendid strategies to address demanding situations, fostering a more super paintings surroundings.

Interpersonal Effectiveness in Teamwork:

DBT Principle: Apply effective conversation and collaboration abilities.

Application: Clearly speak your thoughts, actively pay attention to others, and provide high quality comments. Use interpersonal effectiveness abilties to navigate place of work dynamics, fostering a more cohesive and green corporation.

Distress Tolerance in High-Pressure Situations:

DBT Principle: Develop resilience to face as much as crises with out making impulsive picks.

Application: When dealing with excessive-pressure conditions, exercise distress tolerance. Identify wholesome coping mechanisms, are searching out assist at the same time as desired, and avoid impulsive actions that could have terrible consequences in the long run.

Validation in the Workplace:

DBT Principle: Acknowledge and validate your very personal and others' stories.

Application: Recognize and apprehend the contributions of your colleagues. Provide amazing remarks and acknowledgment for a activity nicely finished. Creating a validating administrative center manner of existence enhances motivation and challenge pleasure.

In every relationships and artwork settings, the secret is to constantly study and exercise those standards. DBT abilities can make contributions to more healthful conversation, emotional law, and choice-making, ultimately fostering more excellent and optimistic interactions in severa factors of life. If annoying situations persist, in search of beneficial useful resource from a highbrow health expert skilled in DBT can offer extra steerage and assist.

Integrating DBT Skills for Recharged Living: Mind, Body, and Sleep

Getting sufficient sleep is important for maintaining your elegant health and well being. A healthful sleep time table can beautify your immune machine, lower your danger of diabetes, lower your threat of coronary heart illness, and boom your hobby and productiveness.

Nonetheless, one in three Americans do now not get enough sleep. According to estimates, among 50 and 70 million Americans be troubled by means of a sleep problem, and among nine and 15% claim that their every day sports are negatively impacted through sleep deprivation.

By addressing the underlying purpose of your sleep-associated problems, dialectical behavior remedy, or DBT, allow you to get a better night time time's sleep. DBT may be succesful that will help you in developing a nap time table and in returning to sleep following a nightmare. This is especially important if you have trouble falling asleep at night time due to the reality even small changes on your middle of the night routine may want to have a huge impact.

SIGNS OF POOR SLEEP

Your intellectual health and favored well-being can undergo substantially from horrible sleep first-rate. However, in case you aren't aware of subtle signs and symptoms which include those, it could be difficult to understand the symptoms of horrible sleep: Dry mouth or sore throat; Jaw and tooth ache; New zits and zits outbreaks; Abrupt temper swings and tension; Junk meals and coffee cravings.

All of these signs and signs and symptoms propose that your sleep have end up no longer super. Your jaw ache and dry mouth are signs and symptoms that you possibly have sleep apnea. Sleep apnea is characterized with the useful resource of respiratory pauses that leave your mouth dry and sore inside the morning.

Brain fog can also arise if you have hassle getting sufficient sleep. A disturbed night time time's sleep can reason problem concentrating because the thoughts turns into without hassle overworked. Additionally, this could dissipate your electricity and make you revel in unnecessarily apprehensive or grumpy.

SLEEP HYGIENE

Your bodily and emotional nicely-being are substantially impacted via the use of the amount and top notch of your sleep. However, in case you've had sleep problems for a while, you might not recognize wherein to begin.

By putting in a agenda that allows you to adhere to, DBT can growth the possibility that you can get an wonderful night time time time's sleep. You can manipulate your emotional response to sleep—or lack thereof—with the useful resource of this habitual. This is especially useful if you experience anxiety in advance than bed. When adhering to a DBT software program, you can employ methods which encompass: 9 to zero meditation; frame scans; consolation and wonderful self-communicate.

Make an try and keep your room cool, and use your bed just for napping. This can create a strong, fantastic association among your mattress and sleep time and help you go to sleep a piece faster.

If you cannot sleep in any respect, think about getting up and doing a little easy obligations in preference to lying unsleeping all night. You can sleep better as properly if you could discover ways to pay interest to your body. You might not need 8 hours of sleep and could discover it demanding to force yourself to get extra near-eye than important.

NIGHTMARE

In most instances, nightmares are not motive for difficulty and are a as an opportunity common occurrence. However, you will possibly need to are looking for the assistance of a DBT professional if nightmares are making it tough if you need to fall asleep.

The purpose of the DBT nightmare protocol is to offer you mastery over your desires. You have the strength to control your imagination and to modify the manner you enjoy on the equal time as you sleep. Begin thru assignment self-soothing and rest sporting occasions as coping mechanisms. After you've got received a few resilience, do not forget running with a professional to deal with a disturbing nightmare.

You can start treating recurrent nightmares through jotting down the info of the dream and choosing a awesome decision. Please make sure that this transformation takes area preceding to any horrible activities, and feel unfastened to make use of your creativeness to create exclusive adjustments.

ANXIETY RELIEF

You can better understand the reason of your insomnia and get greater rest by means of consulting with a nap expert. If you need to certainly maximize it sluggish in bed, you may nonetheless want to address stress. Before going to mattress, reflect onconsideration on a few easy stress-bargain strategies, which encompass:

guided imagery, progressive muscle relaxation, and belly respiratory.

If you do enjoy a lousy night's sleep, do not worry about it. Rather, give interest to making changes to experience more energized at a few stage within the day. Think about, for example: Eating quite a few veggies and wonderful proteins; scheduling exercising whilst you feel worn-out; ingesting masses of water; and giving up alcohol.

These smooth steps can assist lessen your strain associated with sleep and growth your strength ranges. See a DBT specialist as a comply with-as a lot as cope with the underlying reason of your sleep issues.

You can decorate the incredible of your sleep with DBT. DBT want to first be integrated into your sleep time table. This allow you to cope with nightmares that maintain coming again and help you nod off. Try a few strategies like stomach respiration, frame scans, and guided meditations in case you're nevertheless having trouble.

Chapter 10: Implementing Dbt For Your Counseling Workout

When it includes implementation and training, counselors who want to include DBT into their very very very own exercising often find out it difficult to recognize wherein to start. Complete, "modern-day" DBT implementation may be costly and time-ingesting. It moreover has the best frame of evidence, which increases the possibility and performance of favorable consequences.

Conversely, counselors might be greater inquisitive about imposing unique DBT techniques (just like the skills education corporation) or converting the prevailing competencies curriculum and headshot handouts. This form of remedy has been referred to as "DBT-informed," and relying on the population and surroundings the counselor is jogging with, it is able to additionally be beneficial. Basic worries for counselors thinking about using desired or DBT-knowledgeable practices are protected in this article.

The four DBT modes

In DBT, there are numerous remedy modalities to undergo in thoughts, every of which addresses one or extra precise abilties of the same old version. These are the four common modes of DBT remedy, although Linehan notes that extra ancillary modes (like remedy and case manipulate) can be used.

1) Skills schooling: Due to its tangible handouts and instructions for organization leaders, the DBT talents business business enterprise is one of the maximum substantially used DBT implementations. It moreover regularly calls for the fewest sources. There is likewise a tremendous frame of research assisting the efficacy of addressing a whole lot of remedy goals and highbrow health signs and symptoms and symptoms and symptoms absolutely via capabilities education. The revel in of capability training is ready and has a psychoeducational awareness. In this DBT approach, customers only artwork on

developing new abilties, enhancing their capacities, and making use of new abilties to different regions in their lives. The 4 capability modules are: interpersonal effectiveness, emotion law, misery tolerance, and mindfulness.

Individual intervals can be used to complete expertise education. But as Linehan elements out inside the DBT Skills Training Manual, it is able to be difficult for the therapist to set recommendations and time desk ability-constructing time inside the recuperation session. Group durations are therefore normally the advocated technique. Weekly classes lasting to 2 and a half of of of hours are ordinary in organization settings. While the second hour is spent learning new capabilities, the number one hour is spent reviewing homework from the previous consultation.

Usually, the modules final among 5 and 7 weeks. But, relying on the necessities of the net internet website online and the customers, the length and layout may be modified. For instance, institution durations may be furnished extra frequently than as speedy as every week or indoors a shorter time frame. Linehan presents that at the same time as agencies can be closed or open, open groups look like the maximum exceptional in phrases of growing talents. In my revel in, even as a contemporary module began out, I (Michelle) closed the enterprise after which welcomed new individuals even as the following module began. Members of the group had been able to collaborate and take a look at at some point of every module as a give up end result.

2) Phone education: It's common knowledge that the maximum rigorous form of traditional DBT is intake cell telephone training. This makes feel on the grounds that counselors can also favor to dedicate all of their hobby to their families and personal time even as they are now not operating, as they spend a terrific deal of power being there for their customers all through regularly

scheduled periods. Counselors may also be concerned approximately their clients abusing their availability to them at any time after hours, mainly inside the occasion that they've a records of urgent goals.

But as a manner to assist customers in utilising the abilties they've acquired in training to their each day lives, Linehan has pressured the charge of intersession education. A capabilities education call lasts for about ten to twenty mins, on not unusual. Linehan and her colleagues thing out that even though the frequency of calls will range consistent with client, it have to decrease as extra time is spent within the software program.

Regarding the use of cellphone requires capabilities training in among lessons, a number of tips are furnished. This framework encourages the client to use their skills in preference to resorting to needless sanatorium remains or existence-threatening behaviors (along with nonsuicidal self-damage). According to Linehan, skills schooling classes with nurses, intellectual health technicians, and special workforce individuals can replace traditional smartphone schooling if DBT is utilized in an inpatient or residential putting.

3) Therapist consultation group: Linehan and buddies stress the significance of supplying therapists with beneficial resource. The consultation group is made of DBT-expert therapists who get collectively as quickly as each week to talk about times, offer help, and ensure treatment fidelity. Counselors who're considering using DBT at their modern web sites have alternatives: they may method an cutting-edge DBT consultation crew within the network or form a modern-day consultation organization.

It may be hard to sign up for a DBT organization, specifically in rural regions. Linehan does issue out that if wanted, organization humans can time table weekly conferences using internet assets. Linehan and her colleagues advise designating a collection chief for people forming a new group on-internet website on-line. A succesful organization leader offers route and continues the institution inspired and focused at a few degree in the course of the treatment. In addition, this man or woman can be beneficial in assigning institution members to awesome roles constant with their talents, memories, and regions of interest. The feature of the consultation group in general DBT is to beautify the competencies and motivation of therapists.

4) Individual remedy: Weekly character remedy underneath fashionable DBT focuses frequently on growing the customer's motivation. A abilties instructor and an character counselor are generally no longer the identical. Since organisation remedy classes are greater psychoeducational in nature, man or woman treatment moreover affords a steady region for the purchaser to machine suicidal thoughts and nonsuicidal self-damage. In addition to a behavioral

approach to first-rate-of-lifestyles, existence-threatening, and therapy-interfering behaviors, the individual therapist in ultra-modern DBT employs dialectical and validation remedy techniques, regular with Linehan's precise text on treating borderline character disease.

General topics to consider

Counselors need to recall some of different factors in advance than enforcing DBT further to the modes. Where DBT can be correctly included into present day-day systems can be determined by using manner of manner of task an preliminary wishes assessment. This consists of evaluating the goal population and the human and non-human resources which is probably available for the course of treatment. Important things to consider are:

Population: Research has indicated that DBT may be useful for adults and youngsters with ingesting issues, temper issues, anxiety issues, and substance use issues, although it have end up first designed for adults with borderline personality sickness. Program improvement and execution may be grounded through way of focusing most effective at the target population. In addition to any ability patron exclusions or exceptions, admission requirements are a essential hassle to recollect. Admission of customers want now not continually be restrained or good sized. It need to, regardless of the truth that, be regular. It is imperative for counselors to undergo in mind how the selected populace addresses the gaps in the community's cutting-edge offerings, together with the deliver of ingesting disease clinics, chemical dependency remedy centers, and ongoing community assist groups. It is likewise recommended to consider any adjustments that would want to be made to the skills worksheets and handouts. There are numerous publications via using Linehan and distinct professionals that communicate adjustments to satisfy the requirements of precise age companies and diagnoses.

www.ingramcontent.com/pod-product-compliance
Lightning Source LLC
Chambersburg PA
CBHW071440080526
44587CB00014B/1935